Schooling for the Real World

Adria Steinberg

Kathleen Cushman

Robert Riordan

With Foreword by Theodore R. Sizer

Schooling for the Real World

The Essential Guide to Rigorous and Relevant Learning

Jossey-Bass Publishers
San Francisco

Jossey-Bass books and products are available through most bookstores. To contact
Jossey-Bass directly, call (888) 378-2537, fax to (800) 605-2665, or visit our website at
www.josseybass.com.

Substantial discounts on bulk quantities of Jossey-Bass books are available to
corporations, professional associations, and other organizations. For details
and discount information, contact the special sales department at Jossey-Bass.

Manufactured in the United States of America.

Library of Congress Cataloging-in-Publication Data
Steinberg, Adria
     Schooling for the real world: The essential guide to rigorous and relevant
learning/Adria Steinberg, Kathleen Cushman, Robert Riordan; with foreword by
Theodore R. Sizer.—1st ed.
      p. cm.—(The Jossey-Bass education series)
Includes bibliographical references and index.
   ISBN 0-7879-5041-6 (perm. paper)
    1. School-to-work transition—United States. 2. Career education—United States.
3. School improvement programs—United States. I. Cushman, Kathleen. II. Riordan,
Robert C. III. Title. IV. Series.
LC1037.5 .S843 1999
370.11'3'0973—dc21
                                                                            99-6487

FIRST EDITION
PB Printing   10 9 8 7 6 5 4 3 2 1

The Jossey-Bass Education Series

Contents

List of Exhibits

Foreword

In the difficult business of serious school reform, especially the "reform" of high schools, it is enormously satisfying when several independently designed initiatives find themselves converging.

Most thoughtful reform efforts at first concentrate only on their own particular ideas and look only passingly at what others may be doing. Their advocates dig in, but, as these advocates build experience, they quickly stumble over useful practical knowledge emerging from kindred initiatives whose overarching commitments about schooling, while originating in a different place, are found to be fundamentally congenial. In time, and when confidence builds, the initiatives overlap and coil around one another, the several ultimately being more than the sum of their parts.

So has it been with the Coalition of Essential Schools and many of the "school-to-work" initiatives, such as those of the New Urban High School Project and of initiatives spawned by Jobs for the Future.

At its start the Coalition was relentlessly focused on the intellectual, the academic core of schooling. The roots of the school-to-work initiatives emerged from different quarters: from the long-standing vocational and technical education movement spawned originally by the Smith-Hughes Act of 1918; from recent focuses on the worker-as-problem-solver (that is, a person who could "think" a constructive way through a workplace which was itself and permanently changing); to seemingly radical notions of secondary schooling necessary to attract and thus persuasively serve a low income, largely urban population. The Coalition spoke of "student as worker"—the adolescent actively grappling with ideas driven by fundamental questions emerging as much as possible from experience. School-to-work folk found these essential questions in the "real" world and used them as the wedge into serious abstract as well as practical learning. These questions, most teachers found, turned out more often than not to be the same. And what the teachers on each side expected in the way of high quality work from the students also appeared to be similar. The melding of these approaches was as inevitable as it was sensible.

Adria Steinberg, Kathleen Cushman, and Robert Riordan have here outlined how these reform initiatives have effectively coiled together and have then put their collective experience into an accessible and usable form. Given its complexity, the practical reshaping of America's high schools will inevitably be a messy business. Steinberg, Cushman, and Riordan bring some order from their experience and thereby provide all of us a big boost ahead.

Theodore R. Sizer
Chairman, Coalition of Essential Schools

Preface

Not too long ago, the director of a well regarded high school received two speaking invitations for professional development workshops taking place in the same city on the same weekend.

One group, a collaborative of Essential school educators, asked him to speak on his experiences putting the Coalition of Essential Schools' Common Principles into practice in an alternative urban public school. The other group, a school-to-work organization, asked him to talk about his school's substantial involvement in learning partnerships with workplaces around his city.

Two fine ideas, the director replied. But his presentation would be substantially the same for each; why not combine the two groups in a joint conversation? From each he met with the same swift answer, "No, thanks." They had different interests, different agendas, not much to share.

In this story lies the essence of a dangerous division that has plagued public education in this country for more than half a century, a division as deeply inequitable as it is unjustified from the point of view of learning.

The false dichotomy between learning (as in school) and doing (as in the real world of work)—between head and hand, as John Dewey characterized it—lies beneath most of our secondary school structures and practices. By dividing students into those who do Shakespeare and those who do shop, schools play out an assumption that many students will end up in unthinking roles at the bottom of society's ladder while a select few will become its enlightened leaders.

This view of education is unhealthy. As has long been true, it perpetuates a class-based system of inequities ill-suited to a democratic society. In the information era, it also reflects outdated assumptions about the organization of work. Though economists disagree about the extent to which all front-line workers will be called on to make decisions and solve problems on the job, the economy does rely for its competitive edge on high-performance work organizations characterized by a flattening of hierarchy and by customized rather than standardized production. Increasingly, jobs that pay well seem to require a combination of knowledge and communication and problem-solving skills.

The dichotomizing of learning and doing also impedes teaching and learning—no matter what a student's aspirations for the future. Research on how people learn calls into question the passive, fragmented, and abstract modes of learning that characterize many high school classes. Teaching for understanding and fostering students' ability to use school-taught knowledge in nonschool settings requires more active, contextualized approaches. Building on Dewey's work, cognitive psychologists in the last few decades have offered theories and research that support such practices. This robust body of work includes Howard Gardner's theory of multiple intelligences, research on the elaborate working memory programs constructed by the brain, and Lauren Resnick's studies of thinking both in and out of school.

Despite the popularity of these theories among educators, old perceptions linger in the teachers' rooms and hallways of our schools. Many high school teachers continue to believe that "applied" indicates an absence of academic rigor and that vocational studies or work-based learning are appropriate only for those not bound for college. Instead of building a common agenda of rigor and relevance, faculties remain divided, sometimes even polarizing around the question of who has the students' best interests at heart.

The current push for greater school accountability and higher standards has the potential to cause deeper fissures along these fault lines. An understandable public concern about the quality of education—translated into new district and state tests with high stakes for students, teachers, and schools—could have the unintended effect of reinforcing traditional models and strategies, while discouraging fledgling attempts to personalize the high school and introduce more authentic and contextualized learning. Such reforms will only survive and flourish if a strong coalition of educators can make the case for them. It is in this spirit and with this hope that we present the ideas in this book.

School reformers stand at an important crossroads. Three major developments—important new work by cognitive scientists on how people learn, a changing economic picture, and a push for equity on the part of reform-minded communities—are intersecting to make possible a real breakthrough in how our students learn.

But as every teacher knows, the machinery of secondary schooling—its programs, schedules, and logistics—can all too easily obscure and even smother the learning that should be at its heart. Learning thrives when school-based practitioners set about building strong relationships with their students, finding ways to collaborate with other adults to invite young people outside the school into a world where they have both an authentic place and a genuine need to learn.

We will describe this work here, making explicit its assumptions and probing its potential for increased student learning. And we will suggest ways schools can use the connections between school and work not to create individual or isolated programs for some students but to transform the structure and purposes of the whole school.

The authors of this publication have drawn on the experience of three organizations that have been actively engaged in efforts to reshape high schools. The Coalition of Essential Schools works toward whole-school reform using a set of common principles that emphasize inquiry, depth, and personalization. Jobs for the Future starts with a focus on the knowledge, skills, and dispositions young people will need in order to succeed in a changing economy. The organization works with schools, districts, and communities to develop comprehensive school-to-career initiatives as a key education reform strategy. And the Big Picture's national demonstration project, "Changing the Subject: The New Urban High School," works closely with five schools that have adapted essential elements of school-to-work reform on a whole-school basis. Each organization brings with it a treasure trove of information about how schools work and how they can better meet the needs of all students.

The intent of this book is to create a conversation among educators, parents, students, and policymakers who should, and yet usually do not, talk to one another. In Chapter One, we review the principles that guide Essential schools and school-to-work reforms. In Chapter Two, we focus on issues of teaching and learning—curricula, assessments, and pedagogies that increase the depth and engagement of students' learning experiences. Chapter Three looks at strategies that are structural—for example, the creation of schedules and small learning communities that afford all students equal opportunity to use their minds well. Finally, in Chapter Four, we review the systemic side of reform—what Fred Newmann, of the University of Wisconsin's Center on Organization and Restructuring of Schools, calls the "circles of support" from school systems, communities, and the government—that must buttress whole-school reform efforts.

At each of these levels, we will identify the dilemmas that confront reformers as they work toward whole-school change. And we will offer a sampling of useful tools gleaned from the best work we have identified. Our aim is to facilitate conversation and experimentation—not through any prescription for reform, but by training our focus closely on students and on the visions, practices, structures, and systems that enable their learning in the company of adults in and out of school.

Acknowledgments

The authors would like to thank the individuals, schools, and programs whose ideas and materials are cited throughout the text. In the spirit of helping others engaged in similar struggles to create better learning environments for young people, members of the Coalition of Essential Schools, Jobs for the Future, and New Urban High School networks gave freely of their time and generously shared ideas and products that represent hundreds of hours of both student and teacher time.

Specifically, we would like to acknowledge the contributions of Larry Myatt (Boston Arts Academy) and Linda Nathan (The Fenway School, Boston); Anne Purdy (Central Park East Secondary School, New York); Vic Leviatin (Woodlands High School, Hartsdale, New York); Linda Quinn (Puyallup High School, Puyallup, Washington); Dan Davis (Hamilton High School, Milwaukee, Wisconsin); Margaret Vickers and Scott Eddelman (Working to Learn, TERC, Cambridge, Massachusetts); Bob Madar (Crescent Valley High School, Corvallis, Oregon) Christy Zarella (East Boston High School, Boston); Charles Jett (The Critical Skills Group, Wheaton, Illinois); Stephen and Mary Agnes Hamilton (Cornell University, Ithaca, New York); Doris Alvarez and Tom Fehrenbacher (Hoover High School, San Diego, California); Elliot Washor, Dennis Littky, and Elaine Hackney (Metropolitan Regional Career and Technical Center, Providence, Rhode Island); Alberto Carvalho (Dade County Public Schools, Miami, Florida); Fran Vandiver (Fort Lauderdale High School, Fort Lauderdale, Florida); Steve O'Donahue (Fremont High School, Oakland, California); Betty Despenza-Green (Chicago Vocational School, Chicago); Jean LaTerz (School-to-Career Office, Boston); Mary Jane Clancy and Cassandra Jones (Office of Education for Employment, Philadelphia); Kathi Mullin

(School-to-Career Office, Boston), Neil Sullivan (Private Industry Council, Boston); Susan Egmont (Protech, Boston); Keith Westrich (Department of Education, Malden, Massachusetts); Jane Millie (Cranberry School to Career Partnership, South Weymouth, Massachusetts); Daniel McLaughlin (WestEd, San Francisco); and Bob Pearlman (Autodesk Foundation, San Rafael, California).

At Jobs for the Future (JFF), Susan Goldberger shared her analysis of lessons learned from the Benchmark Communities Initiative, Hilary Pennington and Mary Ellen Bavaro provided helpful review of numerous drafts, and Sybilla Dorros provided editorial assistance. Long-time JFF professional development consultants Michelle Swanson and Esther Bobowick and research consultant Cheryl Almeida all contributed insights and examples to the text. At the Center for Essential Schools (CES), Amy Gerstein's suggestions, experience, and contacts in schools greatly helped in our research.

Others outside of JFF and CES also played important roles. We especially wish to thank Bob Keough for his written contributions to Chapter Four, Creating Circles of Support.

Finally, we want to thank Warren Chapman of the Joyce Foundation for supporting the idea of collaboration between the Coalition of Essential Schools and Jobs for the Future and for funding the development of this book.

Boston, Massachusetts May 1999	*Adria Steinberg*
Harvard, Massachusetts May 1999	*Kathleen Cushman*
Cambridge, Massachusetts May 1999	*Robert Riordan*

The Authors

ADRIA STEINBERG has worked in and written about schools for more than thirty years. She is currently a program director at Jobs for the Future. Steinberg has authored numerous publications and for five years was the writer and editor of the *Harvard Education Letter*. Among her recent publications are *Real Learning, Real Work* (Routledge, 1997) and *CityWorks* (coauthored with David Stephen), a guidebook for teachers and youth workers on how to involve teenagers in learning and working in their communities (New Press, forthcoming, 1999).

KATHLEEN CUSHMAN has written for more than a decade about education reform, describing the Coalition of Essential Schools in the journal *Horace* and the schools of the Annenberg Challenge in *Challenge Journal*. Her five-volume work *The Collected Horace: Theory and Practice in Essential Schools* was published in 1998 by the Coalition of Essential Schools. She lives in Harvard, Massachusetts.

ROBERT RIORDAN is a long-time teacher, administrator, and teacher trainer. He was named National School-to-Work Practitioner of the Year in 1994. He is project director for Changing the Subject: The New Urban High School, a joint initiative of the Big Picture Company and the U.S. Department of Education.

Two Visions, One Purpose

This is a time of escalating debate about both the purpose and the content of an American high school education. Should effective schooling aim first of all toward economic productivity? Should it place the development of a thoughtful, democratic citizenry at its center? Should it focus primarily on transmitting defined bodies of knowledge? Should the emphasis be on helping students develop competencies for lifelong learning? Few would say that today's schools successfully accomplish these goals.

Over the past decade or more, the Coalition of Essential Schools (CES) and the school-to-work, or school-to-career, movements have made important contributions to the debate—at first, seemingly on different sides.[1]

---

1. Throughout this paper, we use the term *school-to-career* interchangeably with *school-to-work* to describe this movement. Although school-to-work is used in the federal legislation and in several state initiatives, for some it has negative connotations, implying a one-time transition to entry-level employment rather than a career pathway.

Growing out of Theodore Sizer's fine-grained observations of numbing high school routines and the pervasive institutional culture to "do the minimum," the Coalition of Essential Schools began by creating a language and a philosophy that asked students to use their minds well and teachers to raise the bar for intellectual work. The focus was inside the school—on finding new ways to schedule and group students to encourage deeper learning and stronger connections between teachers and students.

The impetus for the school-to-work movement came from a different set of concerns—in particular, increasing public alarm about the large number of young people who were floundering both during and after high school. Early efforts focused on connecting learning in and out of school and on ensuring that students had mentors who would help them find their way to college and careers. Consortia of educators and employers started youth apprenticeships and other work-based learning opportunities with the goal of opening doors to active learning for students whose motivation and interest were languishing in conventional classrooms.

Both these movements have attracted increased attention and support in the last decade. The Coalition of Essential Schools has grown from a handful of committed members to a nationwide network comprising more than twelve hundred schools and a dozen regional centers and networks. The school-to-work movement expanded exponentially when Congress passed the 1994 School-to-Work Opportunities Act, which provided both a philosophical framework and an infusion of federal funds to bolster initiatives in states and local communities.

For the most part, the people carrying out the work of these two movements have stayed in their separate camps. But key resemblances have started to show up in their practices. A growing concern about equity—about how to create access to intellectual work for all students—has led Essential schools to look for ways to situate learning in meaningful contexts. At the same time, school-to-career reformers have realized that mining the intellectual content of work-related learning opportunities requires changes in both classrooms and workplaces and that learning both in and out of school should be assessed against the same high standards and broad learning goals. The two movements, coming from different places, are now facing the same challenge: mobilizing an entire system—its policies, its professional culture, and its partnerships in the community—to achieve the ambitious end of rigor and relevance.

Two Belief Systems

Educators often perceive both the Coalition of Essential Schools and the school-to-career movement as programs designed to carry out the goal of improving student learning. But, in fact, each represents not a program or recipe but a belief system that can be interpreted and customized by schools to fit their own particular contexts.

Essential schools organize their work around the Coalition's Ten Common Principles, which rest on two central beliefs:

- Secondary schools should focus on teaching all students to use their minds well.

- Teachers should know their students well, coach them to learn in active contexts, and require them to demonstrate what they know and can do (see Exhibit 1.1).

Likewise, school-to-career reform groups organize their work around a belief system:

- Helping all students meet ambitious standards means connecting learning in and out of school.

- The world of work both prompts such learning and benefits from it.

- Students need opportunities to learn alongside adults.

- Such opportunities require schools to function as open systems accountable to and integrated with the community.

1. The school should focus on helping adolescents learn to use their minds well. Schools should not attempt to be "comprehensive" if such a claim is made at the expense of the school's central intellectual purpose.

2. The school's goal should be simple: that each student masters a limited number of essential skills and areas of knowledge. While these skills and areas will, to varying degrees, reflect the traditional academic disciplines, the program's design should be shaped by the intellectual and imaginative powers and competencies that students need rather than necessarily by "subjects" as conventionally defined. The aphorism "Less is more" should dominate: curricular decisions should be guided by the aim of thorough student mastery and achievement rather than by an effort merely to cover content.

3. The school's goals should apply to all students, while the means to these goals will vary as those students themselves vary. School practice should be tailor-made to meet the needs of every group or class of adolescents.

4. Teaching and learning should be personalized to the maximum feasible extent. Efforts should be directed toward a goal that no teacher has direct responsibility for more than eighty students. To capitalize on this personalization, decisions about the details of the course of study, the use of students' and teachers' time, and the choice of teaching materials and specific pedagogies must be unreservedly placed in the hands of the principal and staff.

5. The governing practical metaphor of the school should be student as worker rather than the more familiar metaphor of teacher as deliverer of instructional services. Accordingly, a prominent pedagogy will be coaching students to learn how to learn and thus to teach themselves.

6. Students entering secondary school studies are those who can show competence in language and elementary mathematics. Students of traditional high school age but not yet at appropriate lev-

EXHIBIT 1.1. *The Ten Common Principles of the Coalition of Essential Schools.* Used by permission of the Coalition of Essential Schools, Oakland, Calif. http://www.essentialschools.org

els of competence to enter secondary school studies will be provided intensive remedial work to assist them quickly to meet these standards. The diploma should be awarded upon a successful final demonstration of mastery for graduation—an "exhibition." This exhibition by the student of his or her grasp of the central skills and knowledge of the school's program may be jointly administered by the faculty and by higher authorities. As the diploma is awarded when earned, the school's program proceeds with no strict age grading and with no system of credits earned by time spent in class. The emphasis is on the students' demonstration that they can do important things.

7. The tone of the school should explicitly and self-consciously stress values of unanxious expectation ("I won't threaten you but I expect much of you"), of trust (unless abused), and of decency (the values of fairness, generosity, and tolerance). Incentives appropriate to the school's particular students and teachers should be emphasized, and parents should be treated as essential collaborators.

8. The principal and teachers should perceive themselves as generalists first (teachers and scholars in general education) and specialists second (experts in one particular discipline). Staff should expect multiple obligations (teacher-counselor-manager) and feel a sense of commitment to the entire school.

9. Ultimate administrative and budget targets should include, in addition to total student loads per teacher of eighty or fewer pupils, substantial time for collective planning by teachers, competitive salaries for staff, and an ultimate per pupil cost not to exceed that at traditional schools by more than 10 percent. To accomplish this, administrative plans may have to show the phased reduction or elimination of services now provided students in many traditional, comprehensive secondary schools.

10. The school should demonstrate nondiscriminatory and inclusive policies, practices, and pedagogies, modeling democratic practices, honoring diversity, building on the strengths of its communities, and challenging all forms of inequity and discrimination.

EXHIBIT 1.1, *continued.*

For Essential school educators, whose attention is trained on the Ten Common Principles and their implications for school design, the school-to-career policy climate may seem irrelevant or too focused on the vocational sector or a labor-market rationale for education. They worry that the school-to-career emphasis could compromise the intellectual focus at the heart of their philosophy.

For educators who base most of their practice on connecting students with the world of work, the Coalition's emphasis on intellectual depth may appear vague, perhaps even elitist. They worry that important areas of student development will not be nurtured in a purely academic environment and that a substantial number of students will be left out altogether.

In each case, however, these views misread the character of the other approach and the implications for whole-school change.

Much of the best practice in Essential schools comes from efforts to overturn and transform the impersonal and superficial culture of high school in which adults rarely know kids well enough to guide them and classroom studies rarely presume a genuine need to know. Already, many Essential schools—small and large, in urban, rural, and suburban settings—are beginning to turn to the "real world" of work outside school to connect students with authentic contexts for learning. Similarly, schools entering reform through school-to-career approaches find themselves inevitably addressing issues of academic and intellectual rigor.

Rigor and Relevance

Schools that merge the two visions show how compatible they can be. At Fenway High School in Boston, students work on the real problems of the school's workplace partners. To help the CVS pharmacy chain decide where to locate a new store, for example, eleventh graders sought the advice of accountants and architects, researched and analyzed demographic and economic data, made site visits, projected design costs, and presented written and oral reports to company executives. Juniors also rotate through positions in CVS in preparation for senior year when they will complete an internship and research paper based on that work.

At Central Park East Secondary School in New York City, all students in grades eight through ten work in the community one half-day per week, and all students must complete a portfolio from an internship experience to qualify for graduation.

At Reynoldsburg High School, a suburban Ohio school, juniors design local political action projects in which they identify a community issue that interests them and then research it and work toward its solution. To fulfill the school's graduation requirements, they must present and defend their work in a public presentation before a panel of students, teachers, and community members who know the subject in question.

None of these Essential school undertakings were conceived as "vocational" projects, yet all share key goals and strategies with the school-to-career movement. Likewise, when one looks at school-to-career strategies in the many shapes and forms in which they show up, Essential school principles and key practices also leap out.

For example, Brighton High School students in Boston who participate in rotations and internships in the New England Medical Center are indeed expected to be productive ("student as worker") to an extent rarely attained in traditional classrooms. As participants in ProTech, Boston's longest-standing school-to-career initiative, these students take on increasing responsibility at work, where "real-world" standards prevail, as well as at school where they complete a college preparatory curriculum (see the Fifth and Sixth Common Principles).

When students in the field biology program at Crescent Valley High School in Corvallis, Oregon, work with local stream ecologists, water and soil quality technicians, and fish biologists, the teacher, Bob Madar, acts as a coach rather than a subject specialist (see the Eighth Common Principle). He readily admits to not knowing as much as the students do about whether rye grass will act as a good mulch to suppress weedy growth along the river, but he can, and does, ask questions that help guide students as they analyze the data from their site work. He also assists student teams in figuring out how to solve problems that are occurring—such as when a heavy flow in the stream kept the fish traps from working. Relying on mentors in the field for their expertise, Madar is able to model the learner's role, coaching and consulting as the students take new risks.

Issues of decency and responsibility (the Seventh Common Principle) take on new meaning when students intern in work sites such as the New England Medical Center or participate in community ecology projects such as those in Crescent Valley. Students find themselves in a world of adults with a new set of norms to decipher and honor. Often the challenge is how to exist simultaneously in a world of adults and peers, where issues of civility may have different interpretations. For example, in the humanities class in the Health and Human Services pathway at Hoover High School in San Diego, students designed antidrug and antiviolence messages to display on a prominent billboard in the neighborhood of the school. These designs had to speak to and honor concerns of both adult and student audiences.

Although a billboard is particularly public, the work in most school-to-career programs culminates in the most authentic of assessments, public exhibition (see the Sixth Common Principle). And it must pass muster with experts in the field who vouch for the usefulness and quality of the work. Whether working alongside a soil biologist revegetating a riverbank, or alongside a medical technician in the hospital, students feel a responsibility to meet real world standards, which, according to students, are usually considerably higher than those of the school.

School-to-career aims to raise the intellectual level of student work and raise expectations and aspirations for all kinds of learners. In fact, high-quality school-to-work initiatives typically result in students choosing to go on to college or further study, often with more focus and higher career goals than they had before. Some of the most thoughtful school-to-career initiatives have in fact provided more effective college preparation, particularly for low-income and minority students, than traditional college prep programs. A recent study conducted by the Boston Private Industry Council compared a sample of graduates from ProTech, a long-standing and well developed school-to-career program in Boston, to a matched local control group and to all high school graduates for those years. ProTech participants showed significantly higher rates of college attendance and completion. For example, 64 percent of the 1993 ProTech graduates completed a postsecondary certificate or degree in the four years after high school, compared with only 44 percent of the comparison group. Overall, benefits were greatest for African-American participants. For example, 79 percent of African-American school-to-career graduates were enrolled in college the year after graduation, compared to only 53 percent of African-American students in the comparison group. And African-American ProTech graduates who were both enrolled in college and employed earned a mean hourly wage of $8.17, compared with $6.88 for their comparison group.

In curriculum, assessment, and pedagogy, the steps schools take as they decide to adopt the principles of the Coalition of Essential Schools look very much like what we regard as the most important practices of the school-to-career reform movement.

Jobs for the Future defines these practices as follows:

- Using real-world contexts to teach rigorous academics with an emphasis on higher-order thinking skills

- Expanding academic instruction to include problem-solving and other cross-cutting competencies vital to further study and future careers

- Extending learning beyond the classroom through work internships, field-based investigations, and community projects linked to academics

- Providing students with adult mentors and coaches for project work

- Emphasizing high-quality student products through regular exhibitions, portfolios, and other assessments informed by real-world standards

- Offering regular opportunities for students to explore their interests and develop personal plans for future learning and work

Sometimes, in sad fact, terminology creates the biggest obstacle to Essential school advocates perceiving the compatibility of school-to-career reform strategies with the Ten Common Principles, rather than as a program for noncollege-bound students. This problem persists, we observe, even when the strategy is renamed education-to-career, work-based learning, or school-to-world.

Whatever the label used, the connection between the worlds of school and work must rest on broad educational goals, not occupational requirements—in John Dewey's terms, on occupations as a context for learning, not as an outcome. Defined in this way, school-to-career should be available to any student and should hold students to community standards for high school graduation. It should encourage work in and across traditional disciplines. And it should facilitate collaboration among high schools, employers, community members, and postsecondary institutions (see Exhibit 1.2).

These guiding principles bear a striking resemblance to the principles of CES. Moreover, the practical strategies they require for success—from smaller learning communities within comprehensive high schools to flexible schedules and common planning time for teachers and external partners—directly echo the strategies Essential schools use in playing out their Common Principles. Given this convergence, it is not surprising that four out of the five urban high schools identified in a national search by the Big Picture as implementing key elements of school-to-career reform turned out to be Essential schools as well.

These schools have shown that they need not compromise intellectual focus when situating learning in the vocations or

What defining features distinguish work-based learning experiences from conventional schooling either in academic or vocational tracks? The following list of common criteria came from the Quality Work-Based Learning Network, a joint project between Jobs for the Future and the Coalition of Essential Schools funded by the Joyce Foundation.

1. Experiences are structured around learning goals agreed to by students, teachers, and partners that assist students in reaching standards and graduation requirements of the district.

2. Students carry out projects that are grounded in real-world problems, take effort and persistence over time, and result in the creation of something that matters to them and has an external audience.

3. Students receive ongoing coaching and expert advice on projects and other work tasks from employers and community partners. By learning to use strategies and tools that mirror those used by experts in the field, students develop a sense of what is involved in accomplished adult performance and begin to internalize a set of real-world standards.

4. Students develop a greater awareness of career opportunities in the field and deepen their understanding of the educational requirements of these careers.

5. Students develop their ability to use disciplinary methods of inquiry (for example, to think like a scientist) and enhance their ability to tackle complex questions and carry out independent investigations.

6. Students are able to demonstrate their achievements through multiple assessments, including self-assessment, specific performance assessments (for example, an oral proficiency exam), and exhibitions.

EXHIBIT 1.2. *High-Quality, Work-Based Learning.*

callings of adult life, whether professions or trades, academics, or the arts. In fact, shifting from the abstract, "pure" investigations of the traditional academy to cross-cutting applications of knowledge in practice powerfully redirects our intelligences in exciting and creative ways. Rather than eliminating the practical from intellectual life, this intellectualizes the practical, which as Dewey observed, provides "both magnet to attract and glue to hold" student learning.

Teaching and Learning in Real-World Contexts

Given these broad outlines, what does high-quality, contextualized learning actually look like in practice? What strategies can teachers use to open up their classrooms and schools and let students try on different work and civic identities while they learn the concepts, skills, and habits of mind that prepare them for college and careers?

In answer, this chapter considers four interlocking strategies. The first is to involve external adult partners in the learning experiences of young people, expanding their access to the adult world through field studies and community projects. The second is to link this work to the curriculum through broad generative themes, while equipping the students with tools for independent learning. The third is to situate students in the world of work through internships and other forms of work-based learning. The fourth is to support real-world learning by providing contexts, in or outside the school, where students can reflect on the meaning of their work.

Learning Through Projects

"Not everyone who's doing school-to-career even thinks they are doing it," observes Amy Gerstein, the executive director of the Coalition of Essential Schools. Although they may not have reorganized their entire school around the concept, many schools have used senior projects, service learning projects, and other curricular means to link students with the real world.

In the Wise Individualized Learning Experience (WISE), for example, high school students in a dozen or more Essential schools are designing projects that link them with adults in their communities for intensive research and work in an area that interests them. Often a capstone of the senior year, the project involves reflection, journal keeping, weekly mentoring by a teacher, and a final public presentation assessed by a panel of students, teachers, and community members.

Started in 1972 by Vic Leviatin, a teacher at Woodlands High School in Hartsdale, New York, and now coached by retired teachers from a base in White Plains, New York, WISE works equally well with small schools like New York's suburban Croton-Harmon High School, large schools like Pennsylvania's Bellefonte High School, and student populations with special needs, such as those attending alternative schools or the New York School for the Deaf. "I learned more in those weeks than any other time in high school," Croton-Harmon student Erik Ferguson observed after he finished his project.

Many Essential schools also turn to service learning projects to offer authentic entry points into the larger world while maintaining a connection to academic habits of mind. Sometimes, in fact, the schoolwide organizing of such projects itself makes an excellent learning opportunity for student learning. At Puyallup High School in Puyallup, Washington, students run a lunch-hour service bureau and clearinghouse they call S.O.S. (for Students' Opportunities to Serve), connecting some four hundred and fifty students yearly with work-based learning opportunities in the community. The student organizers offer help as well to academic teachers interested in grounding their subjects in real-world contexts, and they visit classes to coach students on the protocols of the work world. In an annual service fair they bring in community providers, showcase student projects, and advertise current opportunities for service learning. "This way we don't wear out our community with too many scattershot requests for student involvement," notes Linda Quinn, the principal of this comprehensive high school with nineteen hundred students, which requires a service component for graduation. "The service bureau students coordinate pretty much everything, working under the part-time supervision of some of our counseling staff."

Project-based learning that in some way calls on the context or expertise of the community is also advocated by school-to-career proponents as a way to introduce a large number of students, teachers, and community or work partners to the principles of work-based learning. In fact, helping teachers develop their expertise in designing and assessing projects is a major focus of Jobs for the Future's work with a reform network of school districts around the country that are committed to enhancing both educational achievement and employment outcomes for students.

"We try to get away from the idea that only the teachers and kids in academies or career clusters can do school-to-career," says Michelle Swanson, a Jobs for the Future consultant working with numerous schools in the network. "You can be an academic teacher, outside of any such program, a teacher of algebra or senior English, and involve kids in a dynamite research project that takes them into the community." In one such project, algebra students in Dan Davis's class in Milwaukee worked in teams to compare the costs associated with various potential sites for a new sports stadium, calculating fair market value with the assistance of local tax assessors.

Joan Becker, a teacher in North Clackamas, Oregon, who worked with Swanson, made what she considered to be a modest change in the assignment of the end-of-semester research paper in her American Studies class. After coming up with their thesis statements, students were advised to conduct an interview with someone who had experience or expertise related to the topic of their paper. Becker found that the interviews made a surprisingly important contribution to the quality of the papers.

As one student said, "Before the interview, I had the pieces to a puzzle, and afterward I was able to put them together. His examples and themes that he brought to my attention did cause me to alter my thesis."

In her own reflection on this process, Becker concluded: "The interview is a vital part of the research process and should be continued. Not only did it provide valuable information on the students' topics, but more important, it gave life to the research process which many students before the interview saw only as a dull, stuffy process of writing down facts from books. Connecting intelligent, articulate, real people to their topics validated their research and provided adult role models and mentors for the students. As a result of the interview, students now see research as a living process, connected to real people and issues, not just as one student stated, 'reading from books, magazines and computers.'"

As these examples show, individual teachers can use project-based learning to improve both the rigor and relevance of their curriculum. But when a cross-disciplinary team of teachers shares a group of students, it becomes possible to develop more complex, long-term projects that allow deep connections between student interests and the issues and texts delineated in the curriculum.

For example, students in the Communications Academy at Sir Francis Drake High School (ComAcad) in San Anselmo, California, spend half of their school day for two years in a combination of academic and technical courses designed to prepare them for college and to help them explore their interests and develop their skills in the field of communications media. Each academic quarter, the ComAcad faculty organize the coursework around a key generative question. The questions are broad and deep enough to allow teachers and students to cover a variety of topics, texts, and activities through their classes in government, economics, humanities, media, and performance. They also allow teachers to frame a project for all ComAcad students.

Every other year, the first-quarter project stems from the question: "How does the communication of ideas influence the democratic process?" (see Exhibit 2.1). Working in teams, students produce video campaign ads and Web pages that highlight a candidate or proposition on the ballot. In developing these media products, students consult both with their teachers and with professionals in the field. On election eve, the teams exhibit their videos for local voters and then answer questions and address concerns raised by audience members. The students are assessed on the depth of knowledge they demonstrate in this question-and-answer period, as well as on their finished products.

1998 Communications Academy (Drake High School)
San Anselmo, California

First Quarter Theme: Communication and the Democratic Process
Key Question:
How does the communication of ideas influence the democratic process?

Government	I	Foundations of American Government
	N	Politics and Elections (government structure, processes, and so on)
	T	Influence and Access (lawmaking, PACs, lobbying, public policy, and so on)
Humanities	R	Orwell's *1984*
	O	*The Hero's Journey*
	D	World Mythology
		Rhetoric, Media, Propaganda
Media	U	Workshops: video, audio, web-page making
	C	Project: video campaign ads, web pages
		Films: *The War Room, Mr. Smith Goes to Washington*
	T	
Performance	I	Workshops: acting
		Production: "Election Night" exhibition
	O	Theater Company: production jobs, fundraiser
	N	

EXHIBIT 2.1. *Integrating Experience and Other Texts.*
Used by permission of the Communications Academy, Sir Francis Drake High School, San Anselmo, Calif.

Designing High-Quality Projects

One strategy that Swanson and others have used to encourage teachers to design such curricular projects is to offer summer workshops that include teachers spending a day or more doing research in the community or in work sites. This helps teachers think more creatively about how they might relate subject matter and academic skills to actual problems that occupy adults in real-world settings.

Still, it is no simple matter to design a project that is thoughtful, rigorous, and real enough to keep students engaged. Besides their academic rigor, the best projects have some authentic value or meaning outside of school, and real-world standards are used to assess their quality. Drawing on Essential school principles as well as the research of Fred Newmann and Gary Wehlage into "authentic student performance," Adria Steinberg has suggested six criteria teachers can use as they design project-based learning (see Exhibit 2.2).

While few projects would fully incorporate all of the Six A's, these criteria serve to remind teachers of numerous ways they can deepen both the rigor and relevance of students' projects.

Although many teachers and parents recognize the value of learning experiences like these, they worry that students will not learn important concepts and content they need (and on which they will be tested). In fact, extracting those concepts from the community or work setting in which they are embedded can be a real challenge for curriculum designers and teachers.

Coalition-inspired techniques, such as formulating "essential questions" and "planning backwards" from desired learning outcomes, are at the core of teacher workshops offered by an unusual curriculum development and teacher enhancement project called Working to Learn. This project was developed by Margaret Vickers, a science educator at the Cambridge, Massachusetts, collaborative TERC. As Vickers describes it, her "mapping backwards" technique involves a simple but profound shift in the way teachers structure learning for students. Rather than beginning with academic subject matter and later asking how it

This list of questions, derived from Adria Steinberg's synthesis in her book *Real Learning, Real Work,* provides a framework used by Jobs for the Future in working with teachers as they plan curricular projects.

Authenticity
- Where in the "real world" might an adult tackle the problem or question addressed by the project?
- How do you know the problem or question has meaning to the students?
- Who might an appropriate audience for students' work be?

Academic Rigor
- What is the central problem or question addressed by the project?
- What knowledge area and central concepts will it address?
- What habits of mind will students develop (for example, concern for evidence, viewpoint, and cause and effect; precision of language and thought; persistence)?
- What learning standards are you addressing through this project (for example, those of the district or state)?

Applied Learning
- What will the students do to apply the knowledge they are learning to a complex problem? (Are they designing a product, improving a system, organizing an event?)
- Which of the competencies expected in high-performance work organizations (for example, teamwork, appropriate use of technology, ability to communicate ideas, and to collect, organize, and analyze information) does the project provide opportunities to develop?
- Which self-management skills (for example, developing a work plan, prioritizing pieces of the work, meeting deadlines, identifying and allocating resources) does the project require students to use?

Active Exploration
- What field-based activities does the project require students to conduct (for example, interviewing experts, participating in a work site exploration)?

continued

EXHIBIT 2.2. *The Six A's of Instructional Design.*

- Which methods and sources of information are students expected to use in their investigations (for example, interviewing and observing, gathering and reviewing information, collecting data, model-building, using on-line services)?

Adult Connections
- Do students have access to at least one outside adult with expertise and experience relevant to their project who can ask questions, provide feedback, and offer advice?
- Does the project offer students the opportunity to observe and work alongside adults during at least one visit to a work site with relevance to the project?
- Does at least one adult from outside the classroom help students develop a sense of the real-world standards for this type of work?

Assessment Practices
- What are the criteria for measuring desired student outcomes (for example, disciplinary knowledge, habits of mind, and applied learning goals)?
- Are students involved in reviewing or helping to establish the project criteria?
- Which methods of structured self-assessment are students expected to use (for example, journals, peer conferences, teacher or mentor conferences, rubrics, periodic review of progress vis-à-vis the work plan)?
- Do students receive timely feedback on their works in progress from teachers, mentors, and peers?
- What work requirements are students expected to complete during the life of the project (for example, proposals, work plans, reflection papers, mini-presentations, models, illustrations)?
- Do students prepare a culminating exhibition or presentation at the completion of the project that demonstrates their ability to apply the knowledge they have gained?

Exhibit 2.2, *continued.*

might be applied to the real world, this approach begins with a real problem that someone needs to solve at work and connects it back to core scientific concepts (see Exhibit 2.3).

After spending at least a couple of days at a work site, teachers develop an essential question—in this case, a question that

The Working to Learn project at TERC uses a model for "mapping backwards" to develop curriculum as follows:

First, plan:

1. Academic standards (concepts and skills that students should know and be able to do; also known as outcomes, benchmarks, learning results, or frameworks)

2. An "essential question" that is
   - Connected to the discipline(s) that you teach and, specifically, could lead students into an investigation that deepens their understanding of a target theme, topic, or set of skills
   - Of actual importance to someone in the course of their work or community lives, creating a "need to know"
   - Interesting to students (if possible, originating in student interests) and within their ability
   - Complex, deep, thought-provoking, and hard to answer, requiring the use of higher-order thinking skills

3. A workplace issue within a business, industry, or community organization accessible to students, related to the subject matter, and possibly including industry skill standards or generic (SCANS) work skills

Next, plan:

Project framework and criteria for assessment: a long-term assignment for students that addresses the essential question and standards; an authentic means of assessing student mastery of the standards with criteria for assessment

Finally, plan:

Classroom and workplace activities that relate to and support the project

EXHIBIT 2.3. *Mapping Backwards to Develop Curriculum.*
Reprinted by permission from TERC, Cambridge, Mass. Copyright 1998 by TERC.

someone in a workplace really asks and which, at the same time, interests students and relates directly to the course subject matter. In Berwick, Maine, for instance, Scott Eddleman's tenth-grade biology students at Noble High School decided to investigate why algae plagued their favorite swimming hole at

Salmon Falls on the nearby Salmon Falls River. This question was of direct interest to them as well as to town officials and technicians in the local water and sewage treatment plants.

It is also a question, notes Vickers, through which students might "come to appreciate the complex interactions among living organisms and their physical environment in a river ecosystem"—an important concept in biology. Their investigation included visits to the sewage treatment plant, consultations with technicians, and performing their own organism counts and chemical tests on the river water. After five weeks of work, students presented their conclusions at a town meeting along with a proposal for stricter controls on the effluent entering Salmon Falls from the treatment plant.

Ultimately, mapping backwards from workplace issues in this way might call for schools to "change the subject," Vickers says. That is, mapping backwards might actually alter the topics of study within a field, such as science, creating new combinations of subject matter that cut across what is now called "biology" or "physics" or "chemistry." The vested interests of the academic world, she argues, have exerted undue (and politically self-serving) influence on school curricula, forfeiting the otherwise rich interaction between abstract text and theories and the world of practical experience.

If the school curriculum remains stagnant, despite major societal changes in the practical uses of mathematics and science, students will fail to see any relevance to what they are learning in school or any connection between school and the world outside its doors. In any case, coverage is a matter of balance—of deciding what the curriculum should include and establishing productive contexts for learning that respond both to exigencies of covering set bodies of material and the adolescent need for connection, expression, and exploration.

Kids as Consultants

In addition to student projects that originate in the classroom and are based primarily in school, some school and business partnerships have developed other strategies that directly link school and work. In her book *Real Learning, Real Work* (1997), Adria Steinberg describes these strategies as creating "something that does not look like school, as teenagers now know it, or like work, as most of them experience it" (page 69). In field studies, for example, student investigations are initiated by work or community partners who act as "clients" and "hire" students to study and make recommendations to them on a specific decision or problem (see Exhibit 2.4).

A good source for such projects is community-based organizations and city agencies charged with addressing public health issues in the local area or agencies charged with protecting the

---

Jobs for the Future worked with East Boston High School in Massachusetts to develop the following field study in its Health Occupations pathway.

The Problem

The East Boston Neighborhood Health Center wants help figuring out the best way to deliver health services to teenagers.

The Process

- Find out what teenagers want. What keeps teens from making use of health care? What matters to them?
- Compare different types of health services (for example, school clinic, neighborhood clinic, mobile van, home visits).
- Zero in on one or two models.
- Investigate potential problems (for example, with insurance).
- Prepare a multimedia presentation for the board of East Boston Neighborhood Health Center.

The Products

- Consultant work plan
- Questionnaire for teens
- Comparison of different health service delivery models
- Initial proposal for a youth-centered model
- New key research questions (for example, financing, insurance issues)
- Multimedia presentation of a final proposal for a model

EXHIBIT 2.4. *Student Consultants Solve a Problem in the Field.*

ecology of an area. At Milwaukee Trade and Technical High School, for example, chemistry students in the manufacturing cluster helped a neighborhood health center to address the issue of lead paint poisoning among young children. After learning the techniques of lead testing and analysis, the chemistry students analyzed actual paint samples brought to school by elementary school students. The health center subsequently used these results to identify neighborhoods with high lead levels where they could then target their prevention and health education efforts. In carrying out the steps of this project, the high school juniors not only reinforced concepts of basic chemistry but they also learned important technical skills, teamwork, and communication skills through sharing their knowledge with younger students.

At Crescent Valley High School in Corvallis, Oregon, field biology students do projects to preserve or improve the ecology of their local area. They work alongside scientists and technicians who work for the local parks authority, the Oregon Department of Fish and Wildlife, and the Agricultural Resource Service of the United States Department of Agriculture. One team of students, for example, worked on a park development program that involved trying to get a flood plain forest established at a local park. Students learned about flood plain dynamics and then designed and conducted an experiment to test whether a particular species of grass would suppress weeds and result in more trees. In establishing these connections, the teacher went to meetings of the Corvallis Parks Board and the Parks Department, asking if there was any project they were doing to which his students might contribute. He also used his own and other teachers' networks. Within several years, he found that people were actually contacting him with ideas of mentors and projects for his students.

Many businesses and community agencies can benefit from students carrying out surveys and other projects for them, suggests Charles Jett, an educational consultant in Wheaton, Illinois, who advocates such field studies as the ideal way to involve students in solving authentic problems. As students define a problem, gather and analyze data, develop conclusions and recommendations, and present the results, he says, they practice higher-order skills while doing work with clear and immediate consequences in the world (see Exhibit 2.5). This is certainly borne out by the experiences of the Fenway High School students who, as part of their pharmaceutical studies, carried out the CVS field study on locating a new store in Boston.

A partnership between the PECO Energy Company, the Philadelphia schools, and the University of Pennsylvania's Wharton School of Economics has resulted in an annual field study opportunity for selected juniors and seniors in three high schools. Mentored by college students, high school students, chosen from small learning communities organized around business and finance themes, spend approximately eight hours a week for ten weeks completing a field study identified by the company. One group of students, for example, studied the feasibility of PECO Energy's setting up a temporary employment agency to help them maintain a full workforce during the summer months. Academic goals included developing research, writing, interviewing, and teamwork and leadership skills.

Learning Through Work

Another key strategy for developing new hybrids of learning and work is to establish internships or youth apprenticeships in which students spend significant amounts of time (either during the school day and year or after school and in the summer) in work placements designed by employers and teachers to maximize the learning potential of the experience. In the best of these, learning plans and projects—jointly negotiated by students, teachers, and work site supervisors—serve to connect the work students do in their placements to academic content and skills.

Through the Cornell Youth Apprenticeship Demonstration Project, which has received national recognition as a pioneering school-to-work initiative, Mary Agnes and Stephen Hamilton have explored the feasibility of adapting elements of European apprenticeship—a system used in countries such as Germany

Phase One: Planning the Project (two weeks)

- Meetings to learn the process and prepare questions for client
- Initial client meeting to hear history, scope of services, background, purpose of study
- Post-client meeting to review notes, draft a confirmation letter reviewing what the students heard and understood and outlining steps. Milestone: confirmation letter
- Preparation of a work plan

Phase Two: Data Collection (three to four weeks)

- Planning for data collection (in pairs, with known customers)
- Finalize interview guide and schedule interviews
- Draft of introductory letter from clinic to patients
- Meeting with adult project coordinator to review the interview guide
- Team discussion of note-taking process; how to be efficient in capturing the essence; use of numbering technique
- Interviews and summaries immediately after each interview

EXHIBIT 2.5. *Conducting a Field Study Process.*
Used by permission of Charles C. Jett, Ltd.

and Denmark that makes work-based learning the centerpiece of education for more than half of the youth population. The Hamiltons deliberately use the term "youth apprenticeship" to communicate their intention to experiment with a rigorous, multiyear sequence of work-based and school-based learning opportunities, providing formal certification of participants' competence.

Although such a system may be difficult to emulate in most American communities, the principles developed by the Hamiltons, which envision students gaining key technical, personal, and social competencies, can add an element of intellectual rigor to the practice of any type of work-based learning, from initial job shadowing or work visits to full-fledged paid internships or apprenticeships. In the Cornell project, as in other internship ini-

Phase Three: Analysis (three to four weeks)

- Development of findings: What does all this data mean? Statements relevant to the issues being addressed derived from facts learned from interview answers (two to three meetings to cull significant points and insights using interview notes)
- Development of conclusions: What can we conclude about this? Statements of closure about issues relevant to the study (must be supported by the facts)
- Development of recommendations: What should we tell them to do? Action steps client should take (must be supported by findings or facts)

Phase Four: Report Writing (two to three weeks)

- Findings chapter and conclusions chapter developed and edited by team and faculty; easel-style format, in three drafts, written during the analysis phase; a preserved record of work accomplished in professional format

Phase Five: Report Presentation (one hour)

- Team members share key findings, conclusions, and recommendations with audience of stakeholders.

EXHIBIT 2.5, *continued*.

tiatives, one strategy for enhancing the learning potential for students has been to engage them in senior projects.

For example, one student working in an insurance company reviewed cases in which policyholders had borrowed more than the value of their policy; the student came up with a procedure manual, standard spreadsheets, and form letters that other people in the company could use. Another student, in an industrial laboratory setting, used computer-aided design software to create a functional design package for electrical services in a new silver analysis laboratory. His work included architectural drawings, schematics, diagrams, bills of materials, standard construction notes, and scope of work plans. The criteria for this work emphasize both rigor (research and academic applications) and relevance (the development of a product that benefits others). (See Exhibit 2.6.)

In a four-year research and development project on youth apprenticeship, Stephen and Mary Agnes Hamilton found that students gained a lot by using their work placements as the basis for senior projects. They suggest the following criteria for selecting a topic:

- It focuses on something that the intern cares about

- It focuses on something that is important in the workplace

- It stimulates curiosity and questions that guide research

- It is researchable by the intern (Information is accessible to the apprentice through inquiry at the workplace and in other sources such as libraries; confidentiality can be maintained if required; costs, time, and expertise are within reason.)

- It connects with other aspects of the occupation and is not isolated or self-contained

- It teaches the intern something new

- It can benefit others

EXHIBIT 2.6. *What Makes a Good Topic for an Internship Project?*
Used by permission of Stephen F. Hamilton.

Overall, according to the Hamiltons, projects are a way to involve students in aspects of work beyond daily routines and tasks and to foster a deeper and broader understanding of workplace issues.

Students completing such projects, the Hamiltons find, perceive their work-based learning to be more demanding and substantial than the usual school assignments. "Normally, English class and projects, I can whip through them and get them done in a week," notes one student. In contrast, she wants her project at Blue Cross Blue Shield, which she has to present to her boss, to be "extra special." As a consequence, she says, "I am working on [it] every day in school. I spend my lunchtime in the library . . . always working on it."

Boston's Fenway High School has placed learning through work at the center of its restructuring effort without compromising its Essential school vision. Fenway is divided into three houses, each linked to a broad career area and to local partners, such as CVS pharmacies, Children's Hospital, the Museum of Science, and Northeastern University. Although students do not begin learning off-site until the junior year, from ninth grade on interdisciplinary academic course work ties in with workplace problems. In the house organized around health professions, for example, students might follow the medical progress of a particular patient, to explore the clinical and ethical dilemmas that arise in treatment decisions, or they might chart the development of a new medicine from laboratory to pharmacy shelf. Then as juniors, from midyear on, students leave school an hour and a half early to rotate through a variety of positions at their work site; a summer job also awaits them there. Seniors spend part of every day on the job; during the last semester before graduation they step into a full-time, five-week internship and complete a research paper on a related topic. Mentors from each institution supervise students on site and often volunteer to tutor them in academics.

The payoff in confidence and maturity is evident, Fenway's workplace partners note. "I have watched students develop from nervous teenagers to doing responsible professional work," observed Mary Ellen Harrison, who manages laboratory services for Children's Hospital and who often hires Fenway students upon graduation.

Some form of internship or mentorship program shows up in many Essential schools as a way to bridge the transition between high school work and further studies. But Fenway stands out because it assesses internships against the same standards for thoughtful "habits of mind" that other course work is held to. These "PERCS" habits—named for how the work demonstrates perspective, evidence, relevance, connection, and supposition—form the basis of a simple and thoughtful rubric, which the school uses to assess student projects including work-based ones. (See Chapter Three.)

Students who are deeply involved with their projects are typical at the Metropolitan Regional Career and Technical Center in Providence (known as the Met), a small school started in 1997 by two long-time Coalition participants, Dennis Littky and

Elliot Washor. At the center of the Met's philosophy is a commitment to helping students discover and pursue their own intellectual interests. In a "learning through internships" strategy that starts in ninth grade, each student conducts an inquiry to find where a particular interest shows up in the world beyond school, conducts informational interviews with potential mentors, and then spends five to ten hours a week for as long as it is productive in an internship.

When outside the school setting, a student works alongside an adult mentor who also serves on the student's learning team along with the parents and school adviser. Together the student, mentor, and adviser identify a real work project for which the student is responsible, focusing on something that will benefit the workplace while building the particular academic skills identified in the learning plan (see Exhibit 2.7).

Among the first group of ninth graders, for example, one student with an interest in social service worked in a hospital where she developed a booklet on anatomy in English and Spanish for use by both health care professionals and patients. Another worked for a local arts organization, helping them to produce a series for community television. A third developed and analyzed a survey of more than two hundred students who had participated in an after-school program run by her employer, a Rhode Island advocacy organization. These students worked on their projects both at work and back at the school, where teachers supported their skill development.

In the Met approach, the school not only places the student in the world but also follows her there; the adviser goes to the workplace and so, in effect, does the curriculum, as the academic content is drawn from the internship experience.

For example, teacher-advisers use the school's guiding questions to help students learn mathematics through their workplace projects (see Exhibit 2.8). Met teachers feel a responsibility not only to cover academic content, but also to uncover current uses of mathematics in the workplace and connect these to student experience and interests.

All students at the Met School in Providence, Rhode Island, compile a portfolio of completed projects through which they demonstrate proficiency in a set of approaches, technical skills, qualities, and personal goals. Projects can arise from students' work in the community or from their personal interests. To organize their work on work-based projects students complete the following template:

1. Describe the project.
   - What is its value to the organization? What need or problem does it address?
   - What will the intermediate and end product(s) be?
   - Who is it for?
   - When is it due?
   - How will it be presented and to whom?

2. What does the organization look for in order to determine the quality of these products? How will this work be evaluated by the workplace?

3. What are the technical skills and knowledge areas required to do this work? (What skills does the school need to work on with the student?)

4. What can be added to enhance the work (for example, adding relevant reading, displaying results graphically, looking at a historical perspective, comparing and contrasting)?

5. What work materials will be drafted, saved, and moved back and forth between workplace and school during the course of the project?

EXHIBIT 2.7. *Organizing a Work-Based Project.*
Used by permission of the Met School in Providence, R.I.

Teacher advisers at the Met school in Providence, Rhode Island, work closely with students to embed mathematics learning in their work projects.

How do observation and data collection help me solve this problem?

Algebraic skills

- A student researching sleep deprivation must interpret graphs he has found.

- A student researching the physics of "lefty" pitching finds a formula that he must use to generate data.

Geometric skills

- A student measures the dimensions and calculates the area of a room to determine the amount of paint needed.

- A student uses a grid system to locate points on a blueprint.

Statistical skills

- A student uses statistical methods to analyze, interpret, and display the results of a survey.

- Students holding a raffle calculate the prize money based on the odds of winning and number of expected players.

All number sense skills are used in carrying out the above skills.

EXHIBIT 2.8. *How Math Shows Up in Real-World Experiences.*
Used by permission of the Met School in Providence, R.I.

To graduate from the Met, a student must compile a portfolio of completed projects demonstrating proficiency in a set of approaches, technical skills, qualities, and personal goals (see Exhibit 2.9). Back at school, Met teacher-advisers work to equip students with tools of observation, reflection, and analysis for learning independently.

Although few schools are organized around internships to the extent that the Met is, schools use a variety of strategies to achieve an integration with the world beyond school. In the Mount Sinai Health Careers Internship Program, for example, Central Park East Secondary School in New York sends a teacher to conduct an internship seminar right at the hospital. In the seminar, students discuss not only their work assignments but

How does modeling help me solve this problem?

Algebraic skills

- Studying population data over time, a student decides that growth can be modeled by the equation P = PO2t.

- From a graph of points showing a price rising over time, a student draws the line that best fits the points and extends it to predict more prices for the future.

Geometric skills

- To find the best way to pack a product, a student creates a physical model of the product and several boxes of different sizes and shapes.

- To approximate the volume of a person, a student represents the body as a series of cylinders.

Statistical skills

- Making statistical assumptions based on AIDS data, a student creates a dice game that simulates the odds of AIDS transmission.

- A student applies the normal distribution model (bell curve) to calculate the percent of the population with a certain test score.

All number sense skills are used in carrying out the above skills.

EXHIBIT 2.8, *continued*.

also such issues as working conditions, gender discrimination, fears of working with the sick and the dead, fatigue on the job, and repetitive stress injuries. The teacher helps them focus on intellectual content and skills, pushing students to articulate their experience, expand their vocabulary, and generate projects that contribute to the workplace. Thus the seminar serves many functions: support, reflection, and preparation for projects, presentations, and assessment. It provides what Paulo Freire refers to as a "theoretical context" accompanying the more "concrete" context of students' field work.[1]

1. Freire, P. "Cultural Action for Freedom." Reprinted in *Harvard Educational Review*, 1998, *68*(4), 487.

APPROACHES TO INTERDISCIPLINARY PROBLEM SOLVING. To graduate from the Met School in Providence, Rhode Island, graduates must demonstrate proficiency in the use of each question below in their cumulative portfolio.

- *How does past or current experience or history help me solve this problem?*
- *How do observation and data collection help me solve this problem?*
  Rather than making conclusions based on anecdotal evidence or opinion, students must support their solutions with unbiased observations and information compiled through research or scientific experimentation. Students must use appropriate statistical methods to design their research or experiment, interpret the data, and make predictions or conclusions.
- *How does modeling help me solve this problem?*
  Models used by the student may be conceptual, physical, metaphorical, mathematical, or graphical. Students must identify the assumptions or definitions underlying a model, the patterns it generates, what parts of the model accurately represent reality and what parts don't, and what conclusions logically follow from the model.
- *How does logic help me solve this problem?*
  Student solutions must be based on sound reasoning, both deductive (drawing conclusions that necessarily follow from given information) and inductive (making reasonable predictions based on patterns noticed in the given information). Students must be able to explain the chain of reasoning used to arrive at a certain conclusion.
- *How do diverse perspectives help me solve this problem?*
  Examining problems from different viewpoints can greatly enhance the quality and applicability of the solutions. Through research and reasoning, students must understand how their "problem" is viewed by a variety of appropriate stakeholders, including those from different cultures, backgrounds, areas of expertise, genders, age groups, personal situations, and so on.

EXHIBIT 2.9. *Drawing Student Learning Goals from Workplace Contexts.*
Used by permission of the Met School in Providence, R.I.

- *How do "trial and insight" help me solve this problem?*

  Unlike "trial and error"—random uninformed guesses at solutions that end after they fail—"trial and insight" is a cyclical process in which every new guess is based on what has been learned from previous trials. Therefore, results are never "failures" but sources of information to be analyzed that contribute to the improvement of the next trial and to progress towards an eventual solution.

- *How does creativity help me solve this problem?*

  Students using creativity in problem solving use their imaginations to invent original products or solutions or use artistic skills to develop aesthetic solutions.

TECHNICAL SKILLS: Reading, writing, listening, speaking, research, organization, number sense, algebraic skills, geometric skills, statistical skills, computer and multimedia skills, artistic skills, graphic skills, telecommunications, conflict resolution

QUALITIES: Responsibility, integrity, self-awareness, leadership, respect, empathy, cultural sensitivity, cooperation, service, physical fitness, perseverance, courage, skepticism, craftsmanship

PERSONAL GOALS: Students will work with their learning team to develop a list of personal goals, which will include levels of mastery beyond the Met's graduation requirements, and will prepare students for their postgraduation plans.

EXHIBIT 2.9, *continued*.

The overall aim is that the learner (and the teacher) should come to know the world through his or her own thoughts and words and to act upon that knowledge.

Experience as Text

We have described a number of approaches to integrating school with the world beyond, from classroom-based projects to the structured, supported internships of the Met and Central Park East Secondary School. All of these approaches treat the world beyond school as a rich context for learning all kinds of content and developing all kinds of skills. "Changing the subject" in this way means deriving curriculum content from the experience of the student, which becomes a text to be "read" and interpreted just as any print or video text might be.

An internship in a theater that is staging *Macbeth* could lead to a deeper understanding of and appreciation of Shakespeare or may open up the intern's interest in the economics of the Elizabethan theater. A student who works in a first-grade classroom may take an interest in children's literature and may analyze exemplary texts or even write some. A student working in building and maintenance in a large corporation may become interested in knowing why the company has a factory in Russia and what the success of that factory may imply for his or her own job prospects at home. By itself, the classroom can be a sterile context; in connection with settings and experiences outside the school walls, it can be the place where the meaning of the curriculum is articulated.

How would one go about such a comprehensive integration in which the "student as worker" encounters a curriculum that is more like a flow of events than a fixed text? What tools do students and teachers need to accomplish and assess this work? In the New Urban High School project, the Big Picture Company has worked with Central Park East and other schools to develop a set of cross-cutting, interdisciplinary tools that help students identify and extract rich academic content from the workplace. In addition to guidelines and templates for project-based learning, these materials include activities for observation and analysis, reflection, interviews, autobiography, and negotiation (see Exhibit 2.10).

When a seminar or other reflective context (for example, an advising group) accompanies the experience, such tools can help students generate material to share with a community of learners. Within such contexts, students discover what is unique about their own experience; they also learn that they have much in common with and can learn much from their peers. As such, the tools address another critical issue: the teacher cannot follow students everywhere and must rely on them to be expert informants.

1. Observing Your Site

   Reserve ten minutes at the end of your site time to write about the day's observations and activities. Suggestions for writing:

   - *Physical surroundings.* What does the site look and feel like today? What kind of room are you in? What is on the floor, ceiling, and walls? What equipment is in the room? What makes this place different from other places?

   - *The people.* Who is working with or near you? How are people dressed? What are they doing? How do they interact with each other and with you? What are they saying to each other?

   - *The work.* What types of work are people doing right now? Does it seem meaningful to the people doing it? Do people seem trained and prepared to do the work? What is and is *not* challenging about the work?

   Reminders for observation:

   - *Details are important.* What seems irrelevant at the moment may turn out to be useful later.

   - *Trust your instincts.* If something stands out in your mind, for whatever reason, write it down.

   - *Avoid judgments.* Record what you actually see and hear as accurately as you can.

2. Thinking About "The Week That Was"

   Look over your journal entries from the past week.

   - What strikes or surprises you about what you wrote?

   - What feels or seems different to you now than it did then?

   - What have you learned in the past week?

EXHIBIT 2.10. *Observation and Reflection at Work.*
From *The New Urban High School: A Practitioner's Guide.* Copyright 1998, The Big Picture Company. Used by permission of The Big Picture Company.

Central to the notion of experience as text is the practice of writing to record and share observations and experiences. In projects, field studies, and internships, students write in a variety of forms for a variety of purposes and audiences. They keep field logs, reading logs, and personal journals. They write lists, flow charts, chronologies, narratives, interviews, dialogues, instructions, letters, and reports. They write to reflect on significant learning experiences, to think through problems, to articulate learning and project goals, and to share experiences with other participants. In this way, writing is a critical activity for connecting school and the world beyond (see Exhibit 2.11).

If adolescent experience is treated as a primary text for reflection, then identity, social relationships, and change are perennial topics. Students, themselves changing, are often pessimistic about the prospects of change in their own work or community service environments—particularly in their relationships with coworkers and supervisors. Rosemary Sedgwick, a former corporate trainer now working as a consultant to schools, has developed a three-stage process for helping students analyze, understand, and act on workplace issues. Students practice the process by role-playing workplace scenarios and then applying what they learn to their own workplace situations (see Exhibit 2.12).

As students become more proactive in the workplace and learn that they can make a difference, they develop citizenship skills as well. Moreover, as Sedgwick points out, the issues students encounter in their workplace experiences are also explored in a variety of academic disciplines and texts—in social studies, literature, psychology, civics, health sciences, mathematics, and other fields.

Approaches such as Sedgwick's help students develop the combination of workplace competencies and academic skills identified by a high-level commission (the Secretary's Commission on Achieving Necessary Skills, or SCANS), appointed by the Secretary of Labor. These are skills that employers believe to be necessary in today's economy and which schools alone and,

1. *Write often, for many purposes.* Students need to see purposeful writing as part of their daily routine. The journal is one way of addressing this need. It also serves as a spur to conversation, as a resource bank for project development, and as a place to record important thoughts, ideas, and reactions.

2. *Write in many forms.* The workplace calls for forms of writing unseen in classrooms, including memos, inventories, orders, incident reports, and training manuals. But since the goal extends beyond mastery of "business English," the range should include free-writing, maps, webs, chronologies, narratives, interviews, dialogues, instructions, newsletter articles, scripts, autobiographical fragments, stories, and poems.

3. *Write for a variety of audiences.* Work- and community-based programs provide authentic audiences for student work, including workplace colleagues, supervisors, clients, and the general public. Such audiences lend an air of interest and support that both inspires and validates student work.

4. *Share the writing.* Students develop as writers when they tune into the work of their peers and see new possibilities for their own writing.

5. *Respond to writing as real and purposeful.* We can approach student writing as we would the work of any writer: What is this piece about? What moves me? How is the piece put together? What questions does it raise? Students can learn to respond to each other's writing in this way, pointing out strengths and asking salient questions.

EXHIBIT 2.11. *Writing as a Connecting Activity.*
Copyright 1997. From *Real Learning, Real Work* by Adria Steinberg. Reproduced by permission of Routledge, Inc.

Rosemary Sedgwick uses role-playing to help students learn a process for dealing with workplace issues. In working with scenarios such as the one below, students reflect on the issue, practice raising the issue with the other person, and engage in problem solving. Later, they may use the process to address some of their own workplace issues.

Scenario: Work-Related Illness or Injury

Carla is working in computer data entry. She is excited about the work, but recently she has begun experiencing severe pain and numbness in her middle and index fingers. Her doctor thinks she may be suffering from carpal tunnel syndrome and has advised her to not use the computer for a while. Carla wants to do a good job at work and isn't sure how to approach her supervisor with this news. She is also afraid that outside of data entry there may not be another job for her at the office.

Your Own Workplace Issues

While no one can predict exactly what issues you will encounter in the workplace, the following steps may help you handle those that do come up:

1. In your journal, explain as clearly as possible the issue you are facing.

EXHIBIT 2.12. *Workplace Issues as a Learning Process.*
From *The New Urban High School: A Practitioner's Guide.* Copyright 1998, The Big Picture Company. Used by permission of The Big Picture Company.

for that matter, workplaces alone, would be hard pressed to develop in young people (see Exhibits 2.13 and 2.14).

Many Coalition teachers and school-to-career practitioners agree on the need for a fresh set of images—not more rows of desks, number two pencils, and prescribed content, but agility, flexibility, and the ability to negotiate the emerging information networks. School need to strike a new balance between academic, applied, and personal knowledge. Placing students in the world beyond school and uncovering the intellectual content there can help us do that.

2. Look over what you have written to get at the facts. Try to weed out your personal opinions, judgments, and assumptions. List the facts, one by one, until you have covered everything.

3. Ask yourself some questions:
- How is this issue connected to other workplace issues?
- How might this issue be seen from the other person's viewpoint?
- What evidence do I have to support my perspective on this issue?
- What are some possible outcomes from addressing this problem?
- Why is this issue important to me? to others? to the workplace?

4. Decide on a possible approach for solving this issue, and write a script for what you will say and do.

5. List the possible responses the person may have when you raise this issue.

6. Think about how you will handle these responses.

7. Role-play with a partner. Practice addressing the person about the issue. Refer to your script and possible responses as needed.

EXHIBIT 2.12, *continued.*

FIVE COMPETENCIES

Resources: Identifies, organizes, plans, and allocates resources

A. Time: selects goal-relevant activities, ranks them, allocates time, and prepares and follows schedules

B. Money: uses or prepares budgets, makes forecasts, keeps records, and makes adjustments to meet objectives

C. Material and facilities: acquires, stores, allocates, and uses materials or space efficiently

D. Human resources: assesses skills and distributes work accordingly, evaluates performance and provides feedback

Interpersonal: Works with others

A. Participates as a member of a team; contributes to group effort

B. Teaches others new skills   *continued*

EXHIBIT 2.13. *What Employers Want: The SCANS Competencies and Foundation Skills.*

C. Serves clients or customers; works to satisfy customers' expectations

D. Exercises leadership; communicates ideas to justify position, persuades and convinces others, responsibly challenges existing procedures and policies

E. Negotiates; works toward agreements involving exchanges of resources, resolves divergent interests

F. Works with diversity; works well with men and women from different backgrounds

Information: Acquires and uses information

A. Acquires and evaluates information

B. Organizes and maintains information

C. Interprets and communicates information

D. Uses computers to process information

Systems: Understands complex relationships

A. Understands systems; knows how social, organizational, and technological systems work and operates effectively with them

B. Monitors and corrects performance; distinguishes trends, predicts impacts on system operations, diagnoses systems' performance, and corrects malfunctions

C. Improves or designs systems; suggests modifications to existing systems and develops new or alternative systems to improve performance

Technology: Works with a variety of technologies

A. Selects technology; chooses procedures, tools, or equipment including computers and related technologies

B. Applies technology to task; understands overall intent and proper procedures for setup and operation of equipment

C. Maintains and troubleshoots equipment; prevents, identifies, or solves problems with equipment, including computers and other technologies

A THREE-PART FOUNDATION

Basic Skills: Reads, writes, performs arithmetic and mathematical operations, listens, and speaks

EXHIBIT 2.13, *continued.*

A. *Reading.* Locates, understands, and interprets information in prose and in documents such as manuals, graphs, and schedules

B. *Writing.* Communicates thoughts, ideas, information, and messages in writing, and creates documents such as letters, directions, manuals, reports, graphs, and flow charts

C. *Arithmetic and Mathematics.* Performs basic computations and approaches practical problems by choosing appropriately from a variety of mathematical techniques

D. *Listening.* Receives, attends to, interprets, and responds to verbal messages and other cues

E. *Speaking.* Organizes ideas and communications orally

Thinking Skills: Thinks creatively, makes decisions, solves problems, visualizes, knows how to learn and reason

A. *Creative thinking.* Generates new ideas

B. *Decision making.* Specifies goals and constraints, generates alternatives, considers risks, and evaluates and chooses best alternative

C. *Problem solving.* Recognizes problems and devises and implements plans of action

D. *Seeing things in the mind's eye.* Organizes and processes symbols, pictures, graphs, objects, and other information

E. *Knowing how to learn.* Uses efficient learning techniques to acquire and apply new knowledge and skills

F *Reasoning.* Discovers a rule or principle underlying the relationship between two or more objects and applies it when solving a problem

Personal Qualities: Displays responsibility, self-esteem, sociability, self-management, integrity, and honesty

A. *Responsibility.* Exerts a high level of effort and perseveres toward goal attainment

B. *Self-esteem.* Believes in own self-worth and maintains a positive view of self

C. *Sociability.* Demonstrates understanding, friendliness, adaptability, empathy, and politeness in group settings

D. *Self-management.* Assesses self accurately, sets personal goals, monitors programs, and exhibits self-control

E. *Integrity and honesty.* Chooses ethical courses of action

EXHIBIT 2.13, *continued.*

Competency	English and Writing	Mathematics	Science	Social Studies and Geography	History
Resources	Write a proposal for an after-school career lecture series that schedules speakers, coordinates audio-visual aids, and estimates costs.	Develop a monthly family budget, taking into account family expenses and revenues and using information from the budget plan. Schedule a vacation trip that stays within the resources available.	Plan the material and time requirements for a chemistry experiment, to be performed over a two-day period, that demonstrates a natural growth process in terms of resource needs.	Design a chart of resource needs for a community of African Zulus. Analyze the reasons why three major cities grew to their current size.	Study the Vietnam War, researching and orally presenting findings on the timing and logistics of transporting materials and troops to Vietnam and on the impact of the war on the federal budget.
Interpersonal	Discuss the pros and cons of the argument that Shakespeare's *Merchant of Venice* is a "racist" play and should be banned from the school curriculum.	Present the results of a survey to the class and justify the use of specific statistics to analyze and represent the data.	Work in a group to design an experiment to analyze the lead content in the school's water. Teach the results to an elementary school class.	Debate the issue of withdrawing U.S. military support from Japan in front of a peer panel. Engage in a mock urban-planning exercise for Paris.	Study the American Constitution and role-play the negotiation of the wording of the free states and slave states clause by different signers.
Information	Identify and abstract passages from a novel to support an assertion about the values of a key character.	Design and carry out a survey and analyze the data in a spreadsheet program using algebraic formulas. Develop a table and a graphic display to communicate the results.	In an entrepreneurship project, present statistical data pertaining to a high-tech company's production and sales. Use a computer to develop the statistical charts.	Using numerical data and charts, develop and present conclusions about the effects of economic conditions on the quality of life in several countries.	Research and present papers on the effect of the Industrial Revolution on the class structure in Britain, citing data sources used to arrive at conclusions.
Systems	Develop a computer model that analyzes the motivation of Shakespeare's Hamlet. Plot the events that increase or decrease Hamlet's motivation to avenge the death of his father.	Develop a system to monitor and correct the heating and cooling process in a computer laboratory using principles of statistical process control.	Build a model of human population growth that includes the impact of the amount of food available on birth and death rates, etc. Do the growth model for insects.	Analyze the accumulation of capital in industrialized nations in systems terms (as a reinforcing process with stocks and flows).	Develop a model of the social forces that led to the American Revolution. Then explore the fit between that model and other revolutions.
Technology	Write an article showing the relationship between technology and the environment. Use word processing to write and edit papers after receiving teacher feedback.	Read manuals for several data-processing programs and write a memo recommending the best programs to handle a series of mathematical situations.	Calibrate a scale to weigh accurate portions of chemicals for an experiment. Trace the development of this technology from earliest uses to today.	Research and report on the development and functions of the seismograph and its role in earthquake prediction and detection.	Analyze the effects of wars on technological development. Use computer graphics to plot the relationship of the country's economic growth to periods of peace and war.

EXHIBIT 2.14. *How Core Curriculum Can Address SCANS Workplace Competencies.*

Changing the Whole School

3

Translated into pedagogical practices, school-to-career ideas and approaches embody—and help build the constituency for—authentic, project-based, and contextualized forms of teaching and learning. But particularly in urban districts, educational reformers are increasingly looking to school-to-career approaches not just as a pedagogical approach but as a lever for change across the school—for example, toward deeper engagement in fewer and more meaningful tasks, smaller student loads so that teachers can know students better, or a curriculum that reflects inquiry across disciplinary boundaries.

At the William Turner Technical High School in Miami, all 2,000 students take an integrated academic and vocational program of study in one of seven broad career academies: agriscience; applied business technology; health; industrial technology; National Academy Foundation/Fannie Mae Academy of Finance; public service/television production; and residential construction. Each career academy has its own strong identity and offers a "two-for-one" diploma signifying its own signature certificate programs in addition to a college preparatory program of study. The idea is for students to graduate with both the experience and certification to enter a career path and with the academic preparation for college. A member of the Coalition of Essential Schools, Turner makes a point of emphasizing the links between its school-to-career approach and Essential school principles (see Exhibit 3.1).

School-to-career reformers can learn a great deal from Essential schools about how such whole-school change efforts can go right and wrong. Reorienting teaching and learning in fundamental ways involves transforming the way the whole school functions, from job roles to schedules to assessment. Such a shift is difficult and often wrenching; it challenges the status quo and must be carried out more or less simultaneously on several fronts. The experience of Essential schools has shown that the size of the learning community and the ways in which it groups students and teachers, uses teacher and student time, organizes subjects, and assesses students all play a part in whether a change effort will succeed.

Small and Personal

Essential schools and school-to-career advocates have pursued similar strategies and faced similar pitfalls in the task of personalizing the educational process.

Knowing each student well is an important Essential school principle, and creating smaller, more personal learning communities has been a key strategy in the quest of Essential schools to achieve more equitable and effective contexts for learning. In Essential schools of all sizes and descriptions, efforts to establish small, personal schooling environments have yielded positive results, encouraging conversation and collaboration among teachers as they work toward more student-centered, active learning in the classroom.

Some very large Essential high schools in New York City, for example, have divided into small autonomous schools that share facilities and professional development opportunities. Smaller Essential high schools, too, have worked to reduce the number of students a teacher must know and to keep students

The William Turner Technical High School in Miami, Florida, sees the links to Essential school principles as follows:

1. Intellectual Focus

Focus: The purpose of schools should be to teach students to learn how to learn, to develop good habits of mind and work, and to develop thinking skills across subjects.

What it looks like at Turner Tech:

- Application of critical thinking skills in technical areas with hands-on learning

- Emphasis on applied learning through Integrated Curriculum Units (ICUs) on environmental issues at school including air, water, and noise pollution problems

- Use of "learning vocabulary" by both students and teachers and reflection on work and learning by students and teachers

2. Less Is More

Focus: Curricular decisions should be guided by the aim of thorough student mastery and achievement rather than by an effort to merely cover content.

What it looks like at Turner Tech:

- Focus on technical programs of study requiring four to six credits to earn technical certificate

- Establishment of a student-run business, BCA Productions, through the Applied Business Technology Academy

3. Universal Goals

Focus: Academics should be a priority for all students. Core subjects are stressed and use an interdisciplinary approach so that students can see the relationship of one content area to another.

What it looks like at Turner Tech:

- Commitment to trackless education with modifications for college-bound and exceptional education students

- Assessment of student exhibitions using rubrics developed by academy teachers

- Community-service projects: assembling and refurbishing bicycles; airbrushing original designs on T-shirts; packaging and delivering goods to needy children   *continued*

EXHIBIT 3.1. *CES's Common Principles Played Out in a School-to-Career Essential School.*
From *The New Urban High School: A Practitioner's Guide.* Copyright 1998, The Big Picture Company. Used by permission of The Big Picture Company.

4. Personalization

Focus: Teaching and learning should be personalized to the maximum feasible extent.

What it looks like at Turner Tech:

- Students choose technical academy
- Academies staffed by teams composed of technical and academic teachers
- Student identity promoted by academy competitions, projects, assemblies, and uniforms
- Participation in summer internships, community projects, and individualized education

5. Student as Worker

Focus: Teachers should model themselves after coaches, advising and encouraging students rather than lecturing at them; students should be "workers" who are responsible and actively engaged in their own education.

What it looks like at Turner Tech:

- Consistent emphasis on SCANS standards and information literacy
- Integration of Tech Prep initiatives; emphasis on technology applications, active learning, and field experiences

6. Demonstration of Mastery

Focus: Students should be passed only after demonstrating proficiency in subjects.

What it looks like at Turner Tech:

- Commitment to performance-based Competency-Based Curriculum
- Demonstration of mastery on district, state, and national tests

7. Tone of Decency

Focus: Schools should foster decency, trust, and high expectations. Parents should be "essential collaborators" in promoting these values.

What it looks like at Turner Tech:

- Modeling of proper behaviors by faculty and support staff
- Emphasis on integrity, trust, and tolerance; peer monitoring of behaviors

EXHIBIT 3.1, *continued.*

8. Teacher as Generalist

Focus: Teachers and administrators in schools should share teaching, administrative, and counseling duties.

What it looks like at Turner Tech:

- Modeling of flexible behaviors by teachers

- Involvement of teachers in counseling and guiding students as well as planning for integrated units

9. Creative Organizational Plan

Focus: The cost of running high-quality schools should be roughly equivalent to that of traditional schools.

What it looks like at Turner Tech:

- Replacement of department heads with academy leaders and core curriculum leaders; institutionalization of new roles, including Information Center liaison

- Career academies, two-hour instructional periods, and integrated curriculum

EXHIBIT 3.1, *continued.*

together in stable and heterogeneous learning groups, whether through mixed-age advisory groups, multiyear "divisions" or "families," or through other forms of grouping.

Adopting the Coalition's call for small learning communities, school-to-career reformers have translated this into a strategy for breaking large urban high schools down into career academies, pathways, or clusters organized around real-world themes. In this type of school structure, students move with a small cohort of peers and a single group of teachers through a course of study that centers on such areas as communication and the media, health care and medicine, arts and humanities, business and finance, industrial and engineering systems, international studies, transportation, and environmental science.

Framed this way, the idea of small learning communities has found a strong footing in a number of urban schools and districts that were unmoved by more generic versions of "small and personal." Large schools find that career clusters make their programs more personal and coherent, and the smaller, more flexible groupings make it easier to collaborate with external community and work partners. "In my twenty years of doing this work," notes John Poto, principal of East Boston High School, "this is the first restructuring idea to really make sense."

A small number of schools have found ways to combine career clustering with other common Essential school practices, such as longer learning blocks and small heterogeneous learning groups. San Diego's Hoover High School, for example, is both an Essential school and a school that has been nationally recognized for adopting school-to-career as a whole-school reform (see Exhibit 3.2).

In their first two years of high school, Hoover students are in a ninth-grade and tenth-grade "coalition," organized around teacher-student families and two-hour blocks for humanities and math and sciences. Students also participate in community service and career exploration activities and projects. In their junior and senior years, students are in one of three career initiatives: the School of Health and Human Services, the School of Business and Communication Arts, or the School of Design and Engineering Technology. Within these initiatives, students do comparable academic course work—related, whenever possible, to applying knowledge to the career area—and they take specialized technical courses. (A health and human services student, for example, can take physiology, child development, or assistant nursing.)

The attraction of small learning communities organized around career themes is not hard to explain. A career academy promises a meaningful context for students' academic work across disciplines, a culture of high expectations derived from real-world standards, and a structure and opportunity for exploring the world of adults. Ideally, in academic and real-world contexts, students explore and master equivalent sets of intellectual and practical skills. They may apply the analytic methods of different academic disciplines, for example, to the problems of the health care system, or they may study the physics of building an electric car. In the process, they also acquire a more concrete sense of the nature of different work roles than casual observation can provide. They come to appreciate the learning that happens in many work settings. And as they develop a

All students at Hoover High School in San Diego, California, follow a pattern of studies aimed at fostering continuity, personal connections, and career pathways from ninth through twelfth grades. The school's "learner outcomes," assessed by portfolio in all grades, reflect the SCANS criteria. Students spend their first two years in one of three "houses":

Ninth Grade Coalition
- Humanities and math or science in two-hour blocks, grouped in teacher-student "families"
- Introduction to Careers unit, including community service and a "Community 2010" exhibition

Tenth Grade Coalition
- Humanities and biology or physical education in two-hour blocks
- Continued career exploration, including career assessments, in-depth community service, guest speakers, and field trips

Second Language Coalition
- English language learners in grades nine through twelve
- ESL courses in levels one to six
- CES and school-to-career focus

The students move on to one of three junior-senior units in which they combine additional core studies with workplace learning experiences and course electives exploring a career theme:

School of Health and Human Services
- Specialized health classes: physiology, child development, psychology, nutrition, nursing assistant work, physical therapy
- Hospital and health intern placements

School of Business and Communication Arts
- Specialized business tech courses: accounting, business careers, marketing, computer applications
- Career preparation and placement with computer and printing companies, law and accounting firms

School of Design and Engineering Technology
- Specialized technology courses: architectural drafting, drafting technology, construction technology, graphics and communications

EXHIBIT 3.2. *Organizing a Whole School Around School-to-Career Ideas.*

network of personal connections to adults in the world of work, they see how adults shape careers.

But, as the Coalition has found, it is not easy to move a school into this type of organizational structure. Moreover, the history of innovation in schooling suggests that unless the whole school participates in such a change, the innovation will not take hold over the long term. Schools that add one career academy at a time, a strategy that may have appeal at the start, inevitably encounter all kinds of problems with scheduling students, scheduling teachers, providing common planning time, and the like. If the whole school commits to the change, on the other hand, it also commits to solving the problems that come along with it.

Recognizing the daunting obstacles to transforming large, bureaucratic, and territorialized high schools, some reformers have chosen to set up new small schools. Schools like the Met, Central Park East Secondary School, and Fenway High School have been able to put Essential school ideas into practice with fewer compromises than in many larger, comprehensive high schools.

Interestingly, many small schools—including those in the Coalition—also come to embrace school-to-career principles and practices. Small schools often begin with a belief that schools should be more personal institutions, accountable to students and parents. Providing a rich educational experience for each student, these educators realize, means looking to the surrounding community as a source of stimulation, interaction, and experience. "You realize as you know each kid better," notes Dennis Littky, codirector of the Met, "that you've got to put them in places where they can learn and grow. We can't do it all at school." In practical terms, these schools also experience fewer of the barriers to connecting with the outside world: the smaller the school, the easier it is to make arrangements to venture into the community.

Learning, Not Training

Certainly the possibility of bringing in external partners from the community is one of the biggest appeals of creating a strong connection between learning inside and outside the school, particularly for beleaguered and budget-strapped urban schools. Such partnerships can bring new teaching and learning resources to the mix and ultimately help mobilize new levels of community support for education.

But bringing in external partners also complicates the picture. On the practical level, it adds a new set of logistical demands to the already complex practical problems of scheduling a school. It also raises the specter of undue business influence, arousing suspicion that the schools will be turned into training grounds for corporate clients. Above all, critics of school-to-career worry that such initiatives close off options for young people, forcing them to make premature and limiting decisions about their futures.

Teachers in well-regarded career academies see things quite differently. "It's just part of learning, not journalism for the rest of their life," says Steve O'Donahue, who started the Media Academy at Fremont High School in Oakland, California, eleven years ago. O'Donahue admits that he started out with more career-oriented expectations for his program but discovered that its effect on students was much broader. "At first I was disconcerted; we were hoping to increase the number of journalists who were people of color," he says. "But even if kids just signed up because it's a cool thing to do in school, we found that it motivated them in reading and writing, which was our main priority."

Still, the Media Academy does open up career opportunities as well. For example, James Black, a former student who O'Donahue says arrived "just interested in sports, nothing else," went on to write a weekly sports column called "Black and White" for the Charlotte, North Carolina, *Observer*.

The Tracking Trap

As much as school-to-career is conceived as a means to enrich and contextualize all learning, it is hard in schools still heavily marked by tracking to avoid becoming just another program, a sequence appropriate for some students but not all. In schools with significant class and language diversity this challenge proves even more important and difficult. Essential school ideas have suffered a similar fate in some schools, where they are seen as appropriate for only a particular segment of students—those who do not fit into any other special "program," like honors, bilingual, or special education.

Which students are viewed as "appropriate" for school-to-career varies by school and by school system. The tendency in suburban schools with a largely middle-class clientele is to view school-to-career as a kind of revamped vocational education rather than as a more effective way to teach academic and applied skills to all. These schools often turn to school-to-career ideas (and monies) as a way to try something new with students who are not headed to the top echelon of colleges and universities. They continue to enroll other students in honors and advanced placement classes where they receive a separate and unequal course of study, which may be impossible, for scheduling reasons alone, to integrate with a career pathway or other community learning opportunities.

In contrast, some large urban systems find that school-to-work is better college prep than college prep. In systems where elite schools draw most of the honors students, comprehensive high schools struggle to offer college preparatory courses. In Boston, for example, many high schools do not offer physics or a fourth year of language studies. Here, school-to-career pathways or academies tend to attract ambitious students looking for a way to gain the academic background, mentoring, and real-world connections that will help them find a path into and through college to a career.

Even urban systems that do not have separate, elite high schools confront the question of whether to allow honors or advanced placement (AP) courses to relegate school-to-career reforms to second-tier status. Several years ago, San Diego's Hoover High School took the bold step of offering AP courses only in extracurricular time slots rather than as a separate track. Principal Doris Alvarez understood the heavy responsibility that came with that decision: she looked to the faculty, regardless of pathway, to prepare students for college-level academic work.

A new organizational overlay on top of a deeply tracked system will not disrupt it but will become part of it. Ultimately school-to-career, and any other school reform, avoids educational pigeonholing only if it infuses the whole school program. Without an explicit schoolwide strategy for addressing issues of equity, Essential schools and school-to-career programs alike may succumb to the old inequities of tracking.

Setting Standards

The decision to divide a whole school into pathways or academies is not in itself a guarantee of either quality or equity. Just as "doing" an Essential school means more than adopting a block schedule or a few interdisciplinary classes, carrying out school-to-career ideas in a meaningful way means more than creating career pathways or setting up internships. And just as Essential schools have used student exhibitions as an organizing principle from which other schoolwide changes follow naturally, schools attempting to connect learning and work have found that fundamental structural changes can devolve from the way they choose to assess learning both in and out of school.

Coherence in a school's curriculum depends in large part on identifying, in Theodore Sizer's famous phrase, "what students should know and be able to do." Arriving at a common set of learning outcomes that is neither vague nor overly detailed—the "universal goals" that the Coalition urges—can be extremely challenging for a faculty, requiring them to rethink assumptions about subject-area content, about what kids of different backgrounds can do, and about who teaches and assesses what kinds of things. Schools choosing a school-to-career reform strategy have to be especially careful to avoid holding some students to traditional standards (in classes such as math, social studies, science, and language arts) while others get evaluated for teamwork, communication, adeptness with technology, and the like.

The first step is to establish common criteria for excellence in learning. Fenway High School in Boston, for example, assesses all student projects and work-based presentations with a simple rubric that uses the school's essential "habits of mind" (see Exhibit 3.3).

When students spend significant amounts of time in community or work placements, it is also important to communicate these standards to the adults who work with them. Central Park East Secondary School is working with the New Urban High Schools project, for example, to outline for work site supervisors the "habits of mind" the school uses as its guiding principles for learning, so supervisors can reinforce them on the job and link them to what goes on in the internship or project.

Students in San Diego's Hoover High School compile an exit portfolio detailing their accomplishment of six learner outcomes (these include habits of inquiry, use of technology, collection and organization of information, communication of ideas, cooperation with others, and lifelong learning). One side of the Hoover transcript lists course work by semester (with *pass* and *no pass* marks); the other side presents a portfolio transcript that assesses the work in each course (on a six-point scale, from "not ready" to "proficient" or "distinguished") according to the learner outcomes. The work itself accumulates on computer in digital portfolios. Hoover's electronic transcript has been accepted on a pilot basis for admission to the University of California system through the California Transitions Project.

To provide an even clearer picture of how well its students are doing, Hoover collects and analyzes a broad range of data: not only student (and teacher) portfolios but also college entry and retention information, comparative test scores over time, the records of students that stay at Hoover until graduation, student and parent surveys, and more. For example, of the 197 graduates they have contacted so far from the class of 1996, 129 are in two- or four-year colleges. Five former students are in trade schools, eight are in the armed services, forty-nine are working, and the rest are at home.

Setting goals and standards—and paying attention to how well students are meeting them—depends on a concerted and continuing dialogue among teachers, students, parents, administrators, and outside partners about what constitutes rigorous

At Boston's Fenway High School, students defend their senior projects and work internships before an audience that assesses their work for the Fenway habits of mind.

Perspective	Evidence	Relevance	Connection	Supposition
• Considers or addresses multiple perspectives	• Organizes work in understandable, compelling manner	• Shows importance of key concepts in information to other larger or more specific topics	• Links concepts and issues with those from other disciplines or subject matter	• Speculates or imagines other issues relevant to this topic
• Demonstrates understanding of subtleties and differences among perspectives	• Shows clear understanding of issues and concepts	• Demonstrates personal understanding and meaning	• Shows applicability to other research topics, disciplines, careers	• Responds to "What if?" questions and changes of circumstance
	• Demonstrates ability to research key issues			
• Other	• Other	• Other	• Other	• Other
_____	_____	_____	_____	_____
_____	_____	_____	_____	_____
_____	_____	_____	_____	_____
• Surpasses	• Surpasses	• Surpasses	• Surpasses	• Surpasses
• Meets	• Meets	• Meets	• Meets	• Meets
• Needs More	• Needs More	• Needs More	• Needs More	• Needs More

Overall Evaluation:

• SURPASSES: Distinguished responses; demonstrates exceptional critical thinking and understanding; answers all questions completely, poses new questions, demonstrates skills and concepts in an exceptional manner

• MEETS: Competent responses; convincing; demonstrates skills and understanding in almost all regards; makes appropriate connections, answers questions completely, clearly, and effectively

• NEEDS MORE: Inadequate responses; needs improvement in several areas; unclear or incomplete; insufficient demonstration of skills or understanding; redo

Please give other comments and feedback on the back of this sheet.

EXHIBIT 3.3. *Assessing Habits of Mind in a Project or Internship.*
Used by permission of Fenway Middle College High School, Boston, Mass.

and authentic student work. Coalition member schools have found that focusing directly on exhibitions and assessments of student work is the best way to prompt that conversation. Teachers also need exposure to exemplars of quality practice that help them reflect upon, evaluate, and modify their attempts to improve learning.

As at Hoover, school-to-career instructional and assessment practices contribute a vital element to the conversation by connecting to and mirroring the standards of the real world of work and professional life. By broadening educational roles to encompass teaching and learning both in and out of school, school-to-career programs foster the kinds of tasks and assessments that lead to complex and challenging student work.

In fact, in developing their own standards, a number of schools have looked to the SCANS competencies, set out by the U.S. Department of Labor in its report *What Work Requires of Schools*. Sensible and succinct, these criteria rest on five competencies (such as using resources well, or understanding complex relationships) and a three-part foundation of basic skills (such as reading and writing), thinking skills (such as reasoning and problem solving), and personal qualities (such as responsibility). (See Exhibit 2.14.)

Other such iterations come from New Hampshire ("cross-cutting competencies" as defined in their competency-based transcript); from New York's state education department (which adds performance standards at the elementary, intermediate, and commencement levels); from Maryland (called "Skills for Success"); from Missouri (the "Show-Me Standards"); and from the federally funded WestEd regional educational laboratory in San Francisco.

Support for Teachers

Evaluating and improving the quality of a school-to-career initiative, of course, includes not only assessing the progress of students against curricular standards but also assessing and supporting the practices of the adults who coach their learning both in and out of schools.

The school-to-career approach is consistent with the Coalition emphasis on the teacher as a generalist whose role is not merely to transmit content, but to put students at the center of the work and help them view it through a variety of disciplinary lenses. Getting out to workplaces helps teachers to do this work. There are a number of ways to accomplish this, some more intense than others. For example, teachers can lead a seminar on-site (as in the Mount Sinai internship program discussed in Chapter Two), act as workplace supervisors, or participate in summer externships.

In any case, teachers need structures to help them work out the many large and small issues that come up when they work towards more contextualized learning. Without deliberate actions to make their issues the whole school's issues, they may find themselves isolated at the margins of school life in several ways.

Tensions often arise, for example, between subject-matter departments and cross-cutting structures such as career academies or integrated courses. And time issues aggravate the situation further. Teachers who are acting as generalists or situating projects in the outside world need time to learn new roles and carry out multiple obligations. If they are to bring in a broader community of adults to work alongside students as mentors and coaches, they also need flexible time in which to do it.

When learning takes place off the school site, moreover, teachers must rethink long-held strategies for working with students. "I cannot ask teachers to go work in remote locations without serious support," says Betty Despenza-Green, principal of the Chicago Vocational School. In addition to arranging more than sixteen hours monthly of professional development for all teachers, she seeks grant support for university teacher-educators to come to the school to provide intensive coaching for five teachers each semester.

Teachers interested in connecting school with authentic contexts have also found it useful to participate in professional development experiences that include visits to workplaces to audit them for learning opportunities that mesh with their academic goals (see Exhibit 3.4).

As we noted earlier, such visits are a feature of professional development workshops provided by a number of different groups. The Northwest Regional Educational Laboratory, for example, is among several organizations that offer tools that educators can use to assess the learning potential in a work site. And Rob Riordan has suggested ways to draw essential learning tasks and concepts in the humanities from workplace situations (see Exhibit 3.5).

Schools and community partnerships can help establish these connections by providing time and teacher training that includes significant exposure to the workplace and practice in

---

When teachers go out to work sites as part of a professional development workshop, Jobs for the Future staff give them this form to use to document what they find:

Skills and Knowledge at Work

Using a combination of observation and interviews, collect specific examples of:

- Technical skills people are using
- Interpersonal skills people are using
- Additional skills or personal qualities the job seems to require
- Applications of mathematical reasoning and approaches in this workplace
- How and where writing and other communication skills are in use here
- What types of materials people read as part of their work here
- How and where people draw on historical, social, political, and economic concepts in their work here
- Applications of scientific concepts or methods
- How art and creative expression fit into this workplace

(Note: You may want to focus your inquiry on several of the questions that are most appropriate to this work site. Try to collect examples re-

---

EXHIBIT 3.4. *How to Conduct a Learning Audit of a Work Site.*

assessing the learning potential therein. States could provide incentives for this kind of training by revising their certification and preservice requirements to include workplace observation and analysis as well as training in curriculum integration and project-based pedagogy.

Beyond Structure

Both in the Coalition of Essential Schools and in the school-to-career movement, reformers have seen schools make major structural changes, such as implementing block scheduling or smaller learning communities, yet still fail to effect real change in instructional practices or the core beliefs that drive the school. Recent large-scale research on school change bears this out. An

---

lating to at least one question of the first three and at least two from the last six.)

Problems and Projects at Work
Through interviews come up with examples of:

- A routine problem or issue people deal with in this organization

- A more complex challenge or problem that required investigation and the contribution of several people

Opportunities and Resources at Work
Through observation and brainstorming:

- Develop an idea of the kinds of activities a student could be involved in here that would enhance his or her applied learning and academic skills.

- Develop one or more essential questions that a student could investigate through this work experience. Be ready to explain how the question: (a) relates to the discipline you teach, and particularly, to what you believe a student should know and be able to do by the time he or she graduates, (b) is grounded in actual problems or processes in the work site, and (c) might capture the interest of a student.

EXHIBIT 3.4, *continued.*

Changing the Whole School   **61**

1. Situate students in the world beyond school.

2. Treat students' experience as a primary text.

3. Create contexts for shared reflection.

4. Practice academic and workplace skills in an adult milieu.

5. Help students encounter the world through publication, presentation, and exhibition.

6. Think of the teacher as inquirer and clinician
   - As an inquirer, the teacher analyzes the work or community service site for its learning potential.
   - As a clinician, the teacher analyzes students' journal reflections for connections to academic content areas.

EXHIBIT 3.5. *Six Principles for Hands-On Humanities.*
Copyright 1997, From *Real Learning, Real Work* by Adria Steinberg. Reproduced by permission of Routledge, Inc.

analysis of the Annie E. Casey Foundation's New Futures Initiative by University of Wisconsin researcher Gary Wehlage and his colleagues found that unless restructuring is directed at a school's core cultural beliefs and values, merely modifying organizational structures will have little payoff for students.

This appears to be particularly true if a reform initiative is imposed by the district rather than arising from the school community's own interest and commitment. Transforming a school's structure in such fundamental ways cannot succeed until those directly involved in teaching and learning go through the arduous process of reexamining their own beliefs, values, assumptions, and priorities. The trick is to develop a planning process that links basic beliefs to structure, pedagogy, and assessment. As Coalition activists and school-to-work reformers know, high school reform does not mean moving from structure to no structure. Nor does it mean tacking on a few pieces to the existing structure, as "restructuring" schools are wont to do. It means inventing new structures and new routines that make learning the central preoccupation of students and adults in the school and that support students and teachers in reaching and demonstrating the learning outcomes they have agreed are central.

Practitioners and other stakeholders engaged in such a process of invention need to find ways to refer back to basic principles again and again in conversations about structure, teaching and learning, and assessment. Both the Big Picture Company, in its work with five urban high schools, and Jobs for the Future, in its work with schools in thirteen communities, use a principles-based planning process that helps practitioners do just that. The process begins with participants reflecting on some aspect of their current work. They then complete an assessment of this work against a set of design principles, including indicators of what one might find in a setting where each principle was being applied well (see Exhibits 3.6 and 3.7). Then, the group selects one or two principles to work on further and considers the following questions in turn: Where do we want to be? Where are we now? How do we get there? How will we know that we've succeeded?

There are two advantages to such a principles-based planning process. First, agreement on design principles allows groups to work from a community of interest. Second, broad design principles permit conversations across structure, practice, and standards. For purposes of planning, Big Picture has found it useful to focus on the three principles that connect most directly to student learning: personalization (How do we assure that each student is known well by at least one adult?), adult world immersion (How do we end the isolation of students from the adult world?), and intellectual mission (What are the cross-cutting habits of mind and competencies to which we hold ourselves mutually accountable?). The three principles can be cross-referenced, too: How are we planning to personalize our adult world immersion, or how will we connect personalization practices with the intellectual mission of the school?

Design Principles: Assessing Your School (Abridged)

For each of the design principles below, we list features one might see in a program that incorporates that principle. When matching these features to your school's program, use the following scale:

5 = Feature is successfully incorporated for all students

4 = Feature is successfully incorporated, but not for all students

3 = Feature is incorporated with moderate success

2 = Feature is in some stage of planning or adaptation

1 = Feature is not yet under consideration

Part One: Principles

1. Personalization: *Create settings where teachers and students can know each other well.*

   ❑ small, untracked learning communities

   ❑ advisory programs for all students

   ❑ support services for students with needs

   ❑ personal learning plans

   ❑ students explore interests and passions through projects

   ❑ adult mentors available to all students

2. Adult World Immersion: *Situate students directly in the world beyond school.*

   ❑ internships and other community-based learning

   ❑ analysis of placement sites for their learning potential

   ❑ student-developed projects contribute to the placement site

   ❑ career exploration embedded in the curriculum and world experiences

   ❑ one-on-one relationships in the work or service place

   ❑ flexible schedule allows for in-depth learning

   ❑ field studies and projects

   ❑ hands-on experiences with technology

3. Intellectual Mission: *Articulate common core goals for all students across the curriculum.*

   ❑ teachers communicate and plan around core goals

   ❑ core goals are accessible and assessable

EXHIBIT 3.6. *Principles-Based Planning: A School Assessment Sheet.*
From *The New Urban High School: A Practitioner's Guide.* Copyright 1998, The Big Picture Company. Used by permission of the Big Picture Company.

- ❑ standards are developed and assessed internally
- ❑ assessment focuses on what students understand and can do
- ❑ ongoing collection of data on student achievement and outcomes
- ❑ student and teacher self-assessment
- ❑ program qualifies all students for four-year college
- ❑ elimination of tracking

4. Contexts for Reflection: *Provide integrated, reflective contexts for students.*
   - ❑ reflection as a fundamental academic routine
   - ❑ internship seminars, advisories, other reflective contexts
   - ❑ internship and other academic journals
   - ❑ student and teacher portfolios
   - ❑ regular exhibitions of student work and reflections
   - ❑ work experience connects with academics and vice versa

5. Community Partnership: *Include family and community in program development, implementation, and assessment.*
   - ❑ family and partners as members of design team
   - ❑ family joins in developing learning plans and viewing student work
   - ❑ team planning and teaching across institutions
   - ❑ use of community resources for learning
   - ❑ curriculum addresses and contributes to community needs
   - ❑ articulation agreements: dual credit, advanced standing, etc.
   - ❑ public engagement activities

6. Teacher as Designer: *Place teachers in decision-making roles.*
   - ❑ common planning time for teacher teams
   - ❑ teachers in leadership roles
   - ❑ integration of curriculum across all subject areas
   - ❑ support and development of effective small group process
   - ❑ support and resources for teachers' learning

Part Two: Vision

Looking at your school overall:

1. Are your curriculum and pedagogy structured so as to make adult work and adult learning visible and tangible to all students?

continued

EXHIBIT 3.6, *continued.*

2. Does your school treat occupation as a context for learning rather than an outcome?
3. Do you ensure that each student is known well by at least one adult in your school?
4. Is this a place where teachers can and do learn?
5. Does your school collect reliable, longitudinal data on post-secondary outcomes?

EXHIBIT 3.6, *continued.*
From *Seeing the Future: A Planning Guide for High Schools.* Copyright 1999, The Big Picture Company.

This is tough work without easy answers. But some of the most innovative school designers in Essential schools and elsewhere have based their vision on contextualized, real-world learning that aims for intellectual depth. They have translated their instructional philosophy into a clear, measurable set of organizational and instructional practices that schools and partners are responsible for implementing. And they have kept before them one central aim: to move beyond isolated pockets of innovative practice to enrich every student's learning by changing the whole school.

Because its Connected Learning Communities Initiative works not only with schools, but also with districts and community partners, Jobs for the Future has developed design principles and an assessment tool that each of these groups of stakeholders can use to benchmark its progress. Below are excerpts that illustrate the district and community sections of the tool.

District Reform: The district is organized as a network for reform to implement a plan for school-based, districtwide high school reform. District standards, accountability systems, resources, and sustained professional development are focused on building the capacity of schools to improve instructional practice and student outcomes by implementing whole-school reform aligned with the best practices of school-to-career and standards-based reform.

1 Planning	2 Piloting	3 Expanding		4 Systemic		
Core Principles and Practices	Where We Want To Be and What Practice Would Look Like		Stage of Development		Importance	
Creating a focus on high school reform	• District has a plan and implementation strategy for districtwide, school-based high school reform aligned with standards-based and school-to-career best practices	1 2 3 4		Low Med High		
	• Reform plan was developed collaboratively with and has support of key school, business, and community stakeholders	1 2 3 4		Low Med High		
	• District organizes resources to support an integrated approach to districtwide, school-based reform	1 2 3 4		Low Med High		
	• District supports creation of small innovative schools	1 2 3 4		Low Med High		
Building school capacity	• District office is organized to emphasize technical assistance and support for school-based reform	1 2 3 4		Low Med High		
	• District commits adequate resources to support sustained school-based professional development	1 2 3 4		Low Med High		
	• Professional development is focused on building the capacity of teams of teachers and administrators to carry out the priorities of school-based reform and improve instructional practices and student performance	1 2 3 4		Low Med High		
	• District facilitates sharing of best practices and change strategies across schools	1 2 3 4		Low Med High		
Balancing accountability and autonomy	• District sets clear performance goals and supports school-based innovation and risk-taking	1 2 3 4		Low Med High		
	• District standards, assessments, and graduation requirements are aligned with goals of school-based reform and state standards	1 2 3 4		Low Med High		
	• District reviews and revises policies that are obstacles to school-based reform	1 2 3 4		Low Med High		

EXHIBIT 3.7. *Benchmarking Tool.*
Used by permission of Jobs for the Future.

Community-Wide Reform: Business, community, and higher education partnerships provide institutionalized community-wide impetus and support for sustainable school reform, work-based and community-based learning opportunities, and structured paths to higher education, advanced training, and high-skill employment.

Core Principles and Practices	*Where We Want To Be and What Practice Would Look Like*	*Stage of Development*				*Importance*		
Community-wide impetus and support for reform	• A high-level leadership body oversees institutionalized participation of business, higher education, and community partners in school reform	1	2	3	4	Low	Med	High
	• Business and higher education partners help schools develop performance-based assessments of what students should know and be able to do based on the knowledge and competencies needed to succeed in education and work beyond high school	1	2	3	4	Low	Med	High
	• Higher education partners assist in designing and validating applied learning curricula, collaborate with teachers to improve practice, and incorporate school-to-career teaching strategies in teacher education	1	2	3	4	Low	Med	High
	• Business and community partners provide network of trained mentors, and after-school academic and social supports for students	1	2	3	4	Low	Med	High
Work and community context for rigorous learning	• A strong intermediary organization coordinates connections between employer partnerships and schools	1	2	3	4	Low	Med	High
	• Employers provide career exploration and work-based learning opportunities, including paid internships and summer jobs linked to career paths and academic learning	1	2	3	4	Low	Med	High
	• Work-based learning opportunities are intellectually rigorous and have explicit learning goals and assessment strategies	1	2	3	4	Low	Med	High
	• Community partnerships provide quality community-based learning opportunities with clear learning goals	1	2	3	4	Low	Med	High
Connections to postsecondary career and educational opportunities	• Employers provide employment with career ladders and opportunities for further education or training for successful school-to-career program graduates' careers	1	2	3	4	Low	Med	High
	• Industry sector employer groups develop portable certificates of competence recognized for employment and advancement	1	2	3	4	Low	Med	High
	• Dual enrollment allows students to take college courses and offers credit for qualified high school courses	1	2	3	4	Low	Med	High
	• Competency-based admissions considers performance-based assessments of career competencies and work-based and community-based learning in college admission	1	2	3	4	Low	Med	High

1 Planning 2 Piloting 3 Expanding 4 Systemic

EXHIBIT 3.7, *continued.*

Creating Circles of Community Support

4

A central tenet of the Coalition of Essential Schools is that education reform begins not from above but within each school, with teachers, administrators, students, and parents committing themselves to essential principles of teaching and learning. But a decade of Essential school reform has made clear that to achieve their goals, school people need a widening circle of support from the district, the community, the state, and the nation. Such support does not always come easily but must be won through patient, focused advocacy. This is another area where Coalition and school-to-career reformers could magnify their influence and effectiveness by speaking with one voice.

School-to-career reformers have valuable experience to contribute here. For one thing, they have focused from the start on drawing partners from the outside community into the schools. In addition, substantial support at the state and national levels has also helped them develop systemic strategies that incorporate new ways of doing business at the district and community levels.

The reasons for this wider focus are both practical and philosophical. By definition, school-to-career cannot be accomplished within the four walls of a school building. Linking school to the world beyond is possible only with community-wide involvement, and that involvement does not occur spontaneously. Although the exceptional high school may be able to arrange work-based learning opportunities on its own, for such opportunities to be available throughout a school district there must be a systemic architecture of connection.

Beyond such practical concerns lies a vision of a coherent and connected learning community in which young people engage in purposeful activity both in and out of school. Connecting kids with the community has the potential for changing perceptions of America's teens and forging relationships that are meaningful and cross-generational. Schools could become the hub of a community, revitalizing its sense of itself and contributing to its economy.

But this vision brings school-to-career advocates face to face with the institutional realities not only of individual schools but also of school districts and communities. It is treacherous terrain full of roadblocks and land mines.

This territory is also largely unexplored, as most school-to-career efforts have taken place in single-school partnerships with local industry. A number of school systems around the country have attempted to confront the issues involved in scaling up school-to-career systems districtwide through Jobs for the Future's Benchmark Communities Initiative (now operating in an expanded form as Connected Learning Communities). (See Exhibit 4.1.)

"The bureaucracy of large urban districts, the difficulty of changing any of the standard operating procedures in high schools, the isolation of teachers from other adults in the community, the tendency among employers to see their role in terms of job training and workforce development, not education—these are some of the dilemmas confronted by the communities with whom we have been working," observes Sue Goldberger, who directed the five-year Benchmark Communities Initiative.

These dilemmas arise in the context of the school-to-career experience, but they have broad relevance for whole-school re-

Drawing on the experiences of five Benchmark Communities—Philadelphia, Milwaukee, Louisville, Boston, and North Clackamas (Oregon)—Jobs for the Future has identified the following supports that districts and communities should put in place to promote whole-school change based on school to work:

- A strong leadership body to serve as advocate and guardian of the change process

- A staffed intermediary organization to facilitate employer and community involvement

- New central-office and building-level staff roles (facilitator, implementer, entrepreneur) to organize the change process and help connect learning in the classroom and community

- High common standards for academic and work-based learning

- School accountability systems, standards, and student assessment measures that align with the pedagogy of school-to-career, such as standards that emphasize the use of academic knowledge in real-world settings

- Strategic use of professional development to help teachers implement new pedagogies

- District commitment to collect data needed by schools and their partners to evaluate impact of school-to-career learning practices on student achievement and improve performance

EXHIBIT 4.1. *Key District and Community Practices for a School-to-Career System.*
Used by permission of Jobs for the Future.

form, especially when every school, not just one, needs reform. Sooner or later we must rethink the functions of central leadership, control, and accountability if every child is to get a good education.

Shepherds of Reform

Nothing inherent in the experience of a traditional school naturally gives rise to school-to-career as an education innovation. By design, schools are isolated from the world of commerce, indeed, even the world of adults. In the course of their daily duties, neither teachers nor administrators have any contact with adults in other lines of work—not even for the most part with vendors who supply schools with materials. The routine of school life with its jigsaw-puzzle schedules of small blocks of time rarely accommodates collaboration between individual teachers, let alone between teachers and outside agents.

This conspiracy of routine can be daunting. As a start to breaking through it, some schools identify a person whose job is to coordinate and facilitate the change. In Boston, where ten of sixteen comprehensive high schools have embraced school-to-career as a major component of their comprehensive school improvement plans, most of these schools now have on-site school-to-career coordinators.

These professionals have backgrounds that often include stints in business or industry as well as in education. These school-to-career troubleshooters are that rarity among personnel in schools—staff members with flexible job descriptions. Their main charge is to act as advocates for and protectors of the organizational strategies and pedagogical practices that define school-to-career, keeping the avenues of communication open among the various constituencies involved.

Boston's Brighton High School is moving toward instituting career pathways for all students in grades nine through twelve. The school began with a health professions pathway and has since added several others, including business, media/communications, and Teach Boston, a program connecting academic studies to the education profession. A full-time school-to-career coordinator works hard behind the scenes to ensure that the pathway teams have common planning time, that the various pathways coordinate their recruitment efforts rather than compete for students in the middle schools, and that the teachers have the professional development and other support they need to create a coherent educational program for students in the pathways.

"My job included facilitating common planning time for all three pathways, troubleshooting on all sorts of issues arising for the students in these pathways, and participating in restructuring discussions through the school change team," reports Jean LaTerz, former Brighton school-to-career coordinator now working in the district school-to-career office. "And then, of course, there's hall and lunchroom duty."

In addition to having someone who can manage the internal change process, schools need someone who can spearhead external relations. Recruiting employer partners is a labor-intensive process, especially when these partners are not just providing jobs but advancing the larger educational mission of the school. Even at a small school like Central Park East Secondary School, it takes the efforts of several staff members, including an administrative aide and occasional interns, to organize community service and internship placements for all four hundred students. For a large school system, establishing and managing work site placements is an enormous job, one that may be neither sensibly nor efficiently carried out school by school.

In Boston, this coordinating role is played by the Private Industry Council (PIC), an intermediary organization that has strong ties to both the business community and the schools. The Boston PIC employs four full-time recruiters and, in addition, places career specialists directly in the schools. The career specialist matches students with job and internship placements and serves as a case manager, dealing with issues that arise for the student, the school, or the employer.

But among the original five Benchmark Communities, Boston was the only one with a long-standing, respected intermediary organization external to the district office. This fact contributed to Boston's success in finding the resources to staff both outreach to employers and the in-school organizing of coordinators like LaTerz. Where there is no third-party intermediary like the PIC to serve as the central point of contact between the schools and their business, postsecondary, and community partners, the school district plays a more central role.

The Philadelphia public schools have set up the Office of Education for Employment with an independent steering committee that has helped build credibility with the business community. This office has spearheaded an increase in work-based learning placements from 309 in 1994–95 to 2,218 in 1996–97, along with over 5,000 service-learning experiences. The very success of the district in this recruitment effort has created a new challenge—how to provide staffing to support large-scale, work-based learning. They are currently in the process of reconfiguring school-to-career responsibilities within schools and central support staff and piloting new methods of providing businesses with necessary support.

At this point, major urban districts committed to the school-to-career model seem caught on the horns of a dilemma. Full-time staff are essential to quality and integration with classroom learning, but a staff-intensive model can act as a constraint on program growth. Neil Sullivan, director of Boston's PIC, is hoping that a change in state policy will help resolve this dilemma in Massachusetts. The PIC has successfully pushed for innovative legislation to provide stable, long-term funding for "connecting" activities, such as business recruitment and case management, on a statewide basis. This legislation promises intermediaries of local school-community partnerships one dollar for every two private sector dollars spent on wages for students in structured, work-based learning experiences.

Preserving Academic Integrity

Many skeptics about work-based learning fear that the content of job-site placements will be determined by the immediate needs of employers rather than the long-term interests of students. In such educators' eyes, the more that academic curriculum is integrated with work site experience, the more likely that classroom teaching itself could be distorted into narrow job-skills development.

This is indeed a danger, but one rooted as much in academic faint-heartedness as in employer self-service. School systems that vigorously promote school-to-career have found employers who are receptive to the idea of work-based learning not as a

Schooling for the Real World

shortcut to a job but as an essential element of broader education reform. But employers, no matter how committed to educational improvement, cannot be expected to carry the torch of academic content in school-to-career. Business partners need help and guidance in creating high-quality, work-based learning experiences that turn the workplace into rich learning environments for youth. It is up to educators and outside educational advocates to take the lead in setting and enforcing academic standards in career-based education.

In Boston, ProTech has taken on this task. A collaboration of schools, sixty-five employers, and the Private Industry Council, ProTech connects students in high school career-pathway initiatives to high-quality internships in five major industry clusters (health, finance, communications, utilities, and business services). Employers in each cluster and teachers from participating schools meet together monthly.

Keith Westrich, the former director of ProTech, believes that discussion among adults is essential to the quality of such initiatives. Students can hardly be expected to make connections between classroom study and workplace experience, he points out, if their teachers and supervisors have not yet done so. And, he says, work site mentors, however well-meaning, may have little idea how to play an educational role with teenagers. "These meetings change the way adults think about children," says Westrich.

One result of adult conversations is a list of nine competencies that employers and teachers agree are essential to success in both college and careers. Students are expected to develop these competencies through a combined program of school and work (see Exhibit 4.2).

While some employers are more conscientious than others about using these competencies to assess student learning, the list at least serves as a reminder that ProTech is not just about training a young person to do a job but about providing a meaningful context for learning. Using these competencies as a basis for a learning plan creates, as Westrich puts it, a "tool that drives a conversation about educational goals."

INDIVIDUAL COMPETENCIES

1. *Communication and Literacy*

   The student demonstrates the ability to speak, listen, read, and write to function successfully at the work site.

2. *Organizing and Analyzing Information*

   The student gathers, organizes, and evaluates the meaning of documents and information.

3. *Problem Solving*

   The student identifies problems, understands their context, and develops solutions.

4. *Using Technology*

   The student identifies and applies appropriate technologies.

5. *Completing Entire Activities*

   The student participates fully in a task or project from initiation to completion, using appropriate time-management skills.

TEAM COMPETENCIES

6. *Acting Professionally*

   The student meets workplace standards on attendance, punctuality, dress-code, confidentiality, flexibility, and self-control.

7. *Interacting with Others*

   The student works professionally and respectfully with a diversity of coworkers, supervisors, and customers, resolving conflicts in a constructive manner.

8. *Understanding All Aspects of the Industry*

   The student understands the structure and dynamics of the entire organization, health and safety issues in the industry, and the role of the business within the larger economy.

PERSONAL AND PROFESSIONAL DEVELOPMENT COMPETENCY

9. *Taking Responsibility for Career and Life Choices*

   The student balances demands of work, school, and personal life and takes responsibility for developing his or her own personal and professional growth.

EXHIBIT 4.2. *Massachusetts Work-Based Learning Plan.*
Used by permission of the Massachusetts Office for School-to-Work.

Clear Signals and Active Support

True educational reform cannot be accomplished in a top-down manner. But reform also cannot happen on a systemwide basis without a positive role being played by the district office. It is not uncommon, especially in large districts, for the school bureaucracy to stifle innovation at the same time that the superintendent is calling for new ways of doing business. Mixed signals from the top can be enough to keep school-level educators frozen in place.

Before trying out a new approach, many practitioners look for a signal that the reform direction the school has chosen is compatible with major district policies and initiatives. Exceptional leaders may ask forgiveness rather than permission, as the school reform truism has it, but most schools take a more conservative stance, especially when it comes to large-scale efforts in whole-school change. And for schools paralyzed by past failures and lingering uncertainty, a hands-off policy by the central office is not enough.

For individual schools to make a heavy commitment of time and energy to school-to-career reform, they need unambiguous encouragement and concrete support from the district office. Ambitious plans for professional development get shelved if there are not sufficient substitute teachers to cover classrooms. An on-site coordinator may accomplish little if the school cannot install a separate phone line for calls to external partners. For innovations to succeed (or even to get a fair try), schools need a friend downtown, cutting red tape and knocking down roadblocks.

Several of Jobs for the Future's Benchmark Communities have become more responsive to the needs of schools in transition by establishing central-office directors or coordinators of school-to-career programs whose primary jobs are facilitating school change. In Boston, for example, Kathi Mullin, director of School-to-Career and Technical and Vocational Education, plays a key role in coordinating all technical assistance to the Boston high schools that have been designated as "lead schools" in high school restructuring. In trying to address systemwide restructuring principles, these schools are in the process of implementing small learning communities, many of which are organized around career themes. Mullin's office organizes leadership development and professional development for these schools and has set up a data system for assessing the progress of students in career-oriented, small learning communities.

But this kind of support and troubleshooting will count for naught if it flies in the face of other central-office dictates. All too often districts act primarily like regulatory agencies monitoring compliance with sets of regulations and mandates. And faced with mounting criticism of public education, districts may fall back on traditional mechanisms of accountability that stifle the creativity that might lead to solutions to seemingly intractable problems.

One of the main ways that districts (and increasingly states) send signals is through developing and publishing curriculum frameworks and graduation standards. As the Coalition of Essential Schools has long pointed out, the imposition of standards from above is unlikely, in itself, to result in a rededication to essential principles of teaching and learning. Real standards come, the Coalition believes, when the school's own community of stakeholders goes through the hard work of deciding what they want their children to know and to be able to do and what kind of evidence they will accept that this has been accomplished.

But district and state standards can have a deeply chilling effect if they do not support the new forms of contextualized teaching and learning that the school-to-career approach calls for. Schools know they will be held accountable by the district and state for certain learning outcomes (usually measured by standardized tests), and it is easy to allow anything else to die on the vine. The signals sent by the district—and standards and assessments are among the most important—play a crucial role in setting the boundaries of possibility. To fulfill the educational promise of school-to-career, districts must craft their standards in ways that support and reflect experiential, project-centered learning. Schools are much more likely to pursue learner outcomes across disciplinary domains—like those at Hoover High School discussed in Chapter Three—if the district standard and assessments also emphasize cross-cutting competencies of this sort.

In New Hampshire, the State Department of Education has developed a state career development framework that links career competencies to core curricular areas (for example, communication skills align with the language arts framework, and problem-solving skills to the mathematics framework). The career development framework also includes standards for "individual and social learning" and "career learning." In addition, the New Hampshire Department of Education, in collaboration with four communities in New Hampshire and with Jobs for the Future, is piloting a competency-based transcript that includes not only the usual information on courses taken and grades earned, but also features an assessment of whether the student is proficient in a series of cross-cutting competencies, based on the SCANS skills. (See Exhibit 4.3, an example of New Hampshire's "cross-cutting competency" assessment rubric.)

Common and Uncommon Measures

In keeping with current education reform trends, many school systems now offer schools new, though often still limited, local autonomy with the caveat that they will be held accountable for improved results. Unfortunately, traditional measures of accountability—scores on standardized tests—often set schools up for failure. Unrealistic expectations of sudden, dramatic movement along a single, often-skewed yardstick spur the search for quick fixes and punish educators who pursue fundamental improvements that are slower in coming but more enduring. Under this pressure, many teachers retreat to a "skill and drill" approach. Those who buck the trend may keep their innovations a secret, shielding themselves and their students from scrutiny by building walls around what they are doing.

Schools and school systems need ways to measure progress that recognize and nurture innovation rather than pass judgments based on unrealistic goals and expectations. Accountability works best when it is based on a common sense of direction, agreed-upon measures of progress, and a recognition of mutual obligation.

As the Coalition of Essential Schools enters its second decade, it has asked member schools to help create "nationally shared but locally defined" measures combining objective, subjective, and performance-based data to show how school initiatives support greater student achievement. If schools want to look honestly at how they are doing, they must first identify and prioritize their goals and then select "indicators"—questions for which they can obtain reliable and valid data to follow across categories and over time. Taking the time early on to involve key

---

In addition to their state curriculum frameworks, New Hampshire has adopted a set of cross-cutting competencies, described below. Each competency has an assessment rubric. We reprint below a draft of the rubric for the information competency.

CROSS-CUTTING COMPETENCIES

- *Decision Making and Problem Solving:* Making developmentally appropriate decisions and using problem-solving strategies to investigate and understand in a variety of contexts.

- *Self-Management:* Demonstrating individual qualities such as responsibility, self-management, integrity, respect for self and others, flexibility, confidence, and a willingness to explore.

- *Communication Skills:* Using a variety of methods, appropriate to the purpose and audience, to communicate effectively.

- *Ability to Work with Others:* Working effectively with others, including people from diverse backgrounds, and contributing to group efforts by sharing ideas, suggestions, and workloads.

- *Information (Use of Technology, Research, and Analysis):* Using information-gathering techniques in collecting, analyzing, organizing, and presenting information.

EXHIBIT 4.3. *New Hampshire Cross-Cutting Competencies.*
Used by permission of the Department of Education, New Hampshire.

RUBRIC FOR INFORMATION COMPETENCY
(Use of Technology, Research, Analysis)
Performance Descriptor (from the NH Curriculum Frameworks):
The student will use information-gathering techniques in
collecting, analyzing, organizing, and presenting information.

Judgement Statement	Guidance Notes for Assessors	Evidence (types of evidence that may be assessed, but not limited to this list)
Evidence is gathered on at least three (3) separate occasions across all subject areas and accurately reflects the dimensions listed below.		
Gathering: Evidence provided will demonstrate the student's ability to: • use a minimum of four (4) different types of sources per assignment • use appropriate documentation methods • use time and content appropriate material • show use of a plan for gathering information • use effective inquiry through the interactive communications process	Technology must be used as one of the types of sources. Students are required to use standard documentation formatting (e.g. MLA) acceptable to individual districts.	Interview, notes, journal, observation, video, diary, portfolio, self-assessment, chart, concept map, flow chart log book, essay, oral/written test
Analyzing: Evidence provided will demonstrate the student's ability to: • effectively support a thesis which leads to a satisfactory conclusion • verify the relationship between thesis, supporting evidence, and conclusion • interpret and evaluate source material for validity • use a variety of technologies	Evidence is from a minimum of four (4) different types of sources.	Interview, conference, group discussion, questionnaire, portfolio, reflective writing, worksheet, spreadsheet, outline, sorting, log book, label, model, graph, sequencing and ordering, check list, time line
Organizing: Evidence provided will demonstrate the student's ability to: • formally outline proposed product • use a date filing and organization system • understand and justify use of a particular organizational system	Organizational system can be notebook, portfolio, floppy disk, etc.	Data organizing, Web multimedia presentation, project, demonstration, collage, map, article
Presenting: Evidence provided will demonstrate the student's ability to: • use a minimum of four (4) pieces of evidence to support the main thesis • effectively present the thesis and evidence using at least three (3) interactive communications processes • target presentation to the audience	The same evidence/demonstration may be used to assess this dimension and the visual/audio representation dimension of the Communications Skills Competency.	Video, diorama, cartoon, poster, mobile, poem, drama, model, photo, mime

EXHIBIT 4.3, *continued.*

stakeholders—including the district and community partners—in defining these markers of change may prove the critical step in the success of a school's reform effort.

The Coalition is working on a set of "common" and "uncommon" measures that, taken together, can provide a multifaceted picture of school progress. (See *Horace,* Volume 12, Number 3.) Common measures might include not only test scores but also average daily attendance (for students and for teachers); disciplinary referrals, suspensions, and tardies; graduation rates; dropout rates; and college admissions rates. Uncommon measures might include samples of student work or assessment tasks; satisfaction surveys of students, teachers, parents, and principals; follow-up studies of graduates; indicators of personalization, such as teacher-student loads and the percentage of teachers on teams with students in common; and the percentage of students in activities that link schooling with the outside community.

In Illinois, the Alliance of Essential Schools came up with seven categories of information that reflect the Ten Common Principles so member schools can keep track of their progress. And in a more empirical and scholarly setting, a list of indicators for "restructuring practices" came in 1995 from a set of longitudinal studies conducted by the U.S. Department of Education's research center, directed by Fred Newmann at the University of Wisconsin.

In the end, any documentation effort worth its salt will put good questions at its center, answering them with as many different kinds of evidence as possible. At the level closest to students, it will seek out evidence that kids are engaged in meaningful work and experiences. It will insist on longitudinal measures of school effectiveness based on students' success in the world beyond school. At the district and state levels, it will look for policies and spending decisions that support schools' capacity to make changes and provide equitable opportunities for student learning. The synergy among these factors complicates the task of documenting school progress, but it also keeps it honest. (See *Horace,* Volume 14, Number 2 for a longer discussion of how Essential schools are demonstrating student performance.)

Several states have piloted a School Quality Review initiative, a two-part process of self-study and external review that takes place in a five-year cycle. An internal review team involves the whole faculty in a four-year assessment of teaching and learning and prepares a school portfolio to document its collective perspective, questions, and expectations. Teachers and administrators from other districts as well as parents and community members visit the school for an intensive week of observation, interviews, and looking at student work; they then write a report to the staff. The upshot is a faculty-generated plan of action aimed at continuous improvement and building a culture of ongoing review.

Coalition member schools in New York City also engage in a process of "lateral," or mutual, accountability in which small networks of schools agree to review each other's student exhibitions and portfolios according to common standards of excellence and give regular feedback in the role of "critical friends."

Benchmarking School-to-Career Reforms

The Benchmark Communities Initiative developed a form of reciprocal accountability that emphasizes learning outside of school as well as inside. School and business leaders agree to a definition of what constitutes a quality, work-based learning experience for students (see Exhibit 1.2) as a prelude to documenting (and celebrating) steps toward that goal (see Exhibit 4.4).

This commitment to benchmarking school-to-career expedites modifications in the school system's student data system so it can flag students who are in combined programs of work and study. This is a critical first step to examining how students in such programs compare to other students on such standard measures as grade point average, attendance, and dropout rate.

In addition, surveys—of students, teachers, and work supervisors—provide data on the level of implementation of teaching practices as well as on how students and supervisors view their

How do you know if your community is making progress toward improving educational and career opportunities for young people? In Jobs for the Future's five Benchmark Communities, participants charted these things:

- The percentage of high schools that have eliminated the general or noncollege-bound track

- The number of schools that are implementing school-to-career on a whole-school basis to improve teaching and learning

- The percentage of students in designated schools who are participating in an intensive school-to-career program of study

- The number of employers providing different levels of work-based learning experiences to students and teachers

- The number of teachers reporting changed teaching practices in their classrooms and the extent of use of these new practices

- Student academic progress on a range of measures (portfolios, grades, graduation rates, test scores)

- Student enrollment in and completion of postsecondary educational programs and employment in high-skill jobs

EXHIBIT 4.4. *Benchmarks of Community Progress.*
Used by permission of Jobs for the Future.

experiences. In Boston, the Private Industry Council also conducts surveys of graduates of its initiatives to find postsecondary enrollment and retention rates. And schools are not the only ones held accountable. In agreeing to a definition of what constitutes a quality experience for kids, employers assume an obligation to bring a certain number of work-based learning opportunities to the table. They agree to assess whether they are meeting quality standards at the work site and to measure the learning taking place there.

For these measures of accountability to hold their own against one-size-fits-all standardized tests, there must be community support for the direction they set and the measures they employ to chart progress. Boston and Philadelphia have created leadership councils made up of influential figures such as school superintendents, district directors, community mediators that mediate between schools and workplaces, local corporate chief executive officers, leaders of local postsecondary institutions, and directors of community-based organizations and agencies.

The leadership groups in several of these communities have worked with Jobs for the Future to develop indices for assessing the level of intensity of both school and work components. This allows the group to look at traditional measures of student progress—such as employer evaluations and standardized test scores—alongside data on the quality of the experience students are actually having (see Exhibit 4.5).

The steering committee in Boston has also supported development of assessment rubrics geared to the district's learning standards as well as the nine competencies employers use to frame work-based learning plans (see Exhibit 4.2). Such tools both measure and promote the rigor of work-based learning experiences. This year teachers in selected schools are experimenting with using these same rubrics to assess applied learning in their classrooms.

Such leadership groups can shield fledgling initiatives from premature judgment as school-based reforms take hold and can also exert leverage through their own resources and influence. In Boston, leadership group members are now convinced of the willingness of the school district to collect data in new ways and to use that data to inform ongoing reform. They have encouraged employers to provide hundreds of high-quality work site and community learning opportunities for students, mentoring and college scholarship support for students and graduates, and access to good first jobs for high school graduates.

The School-to-Career Leadership Council in Philadelphia has taken similar action to mobilize financial and political capital in the schools. It has established three subcommittees: one on generating employer involvement in school reform, one on promoting public understanding and acceptance of school reform, and one on generating the resources needed to carry reform forward. Thus far the contributions have been substantial; employers support mentoring and work-based learning placements for

In Boston high schools, the main strategy for implementing school-to-work as whole-school change is through the creation of career pathways—multiyear sequences of academic and applied courses and work-based learning experiences. Working with Jobs for the Future, a leadership group of employers and educators has begun to document the level and intensity of career pathway development.

SCHOOL-BASED

Components of Established Pathways

- How many courses and grade levels are part of the pathway?

- How many core academic courses are integrated with pathway courses?

- What field experiences (internships, work placements, community service, etc.) are required of students in the pathway?

Uses of Applied Learning in Class

- Does the teacher use project-based learning as an approach? How often? How many projects do students work on in the course? For how long? How many are collaborations with outside organizations?

- Does the teacher use other learning activities that connect to solving real-world problems? How often? How many and what types? With respect to which subjects?

- Does the teacher use activities (journals, discussions) that ask students to integrate their school-based and work-based experiences? How often? How many and what types?

Assessment Practices

- Which graduation portfolio requirements does each pathway course address?

- Do students complete products with real work significance?

- Which alternative assessment methods are used?

Connection to Postsecondary Options

- Which and how many pathway courses qualify for college credit or course requirements?

- Are students enrolled in dual-enrollment (high school and college) programs?

- Do they have opportunities to participate in college-sponsored activities?

EXHIBIT 4.5. *Boston School-to-Career Initiative: Measuring the Level and Intensity of Career Pathways Development.*
Used by permission of Jobs for the Future.

PRIMARY SOURCES OF DATA (School-Based)

- District and school-to-career data
- Survey of all career pathway teachers
- Survey of all career pathway seniors
- Survey of all career pathway sophomores
- Interviews of key school-to-career staff
- Review of career pathway materials

WORK-BASED

Work Frequency, Duration, and Status

- How many days a week are students at the work site? For how long each day?
- What is their employment status (paid, unpaid, intern)?
- Is the field experience part of a sequence of structured work experiences for each grade?

Role of Supervisor

- What is the nature and extent of supervision?
- How often are students' experiences assessed by the supervisor?

Establishing Learning Goals

- To what degree is the work experience structured around the eleven school-to-career competencies?
- Are learning goals put in writing as part of a student's specific learning plan?
- Is that plan or other goals statement assessed, reviewed, and revised? How often? By what process and by whom? How is the resulting information used?

Uses of Project-Based Learning at Work

- Do students work on projects at the work site? How many? Of what duration?
- Do those projects meet the criteria for high-quality learning? (See Exhibit 1.2.)

PRIMARY SOURCES OF DATA (Work-Based)

- Private Industry Council data
- Survey of all career pathway seniors
- Survey of employers
- Supervisor assessments
- Review of learning plans

EXHIBIT 4.5, *continued.*

Creating Circles of Community Support

students as well as professional development opportunities for teachers and administrators.

The State Role

If the district's bureaucratic and seemingly arbitrary ways of doing business have sometimes felt all too real to educators, the state has always been more of an abstraction. In the past few years, however, as the movement for higher academic standards has gained momentum, state policy has begun to have a much more immediate impact on schools. Increasingly, public schools are operating in a world in which the expectations for what students are expected to know and be able to do have been set by a public body external to the school and the community.

Through passage of education reform acts, development of curriculum frameworks, and in some places, implementation of high-stakes tests, states have become key actors in the education arena. As the dispenser of federal and state dollars, states hold carrots as well as sticks. State policy affects how districts and schools spend Carl Perkins and School-to-Work Opportunities Act funding—both potentially important sources of support for authentic, contextual learning and strategies for connecting school and work.

Yet school-to-career initiatives and other educational reforms remain separate in many states, despite the fact that proponents of both emphasize how vital it is for all young people—not just those competing to enter selective four-year colleges—to get a rigorous high school education. The result, notes science educator Margaret Vickers, "is about as effective as clapping with one hand."

How school-to-career evolves as an education reform strategy varies across and within states and districts. In some instances, rather than using these principles to expand the definition of core knowledge and skills that all students should demonstrate, states and districts shape school-to-career initiatives as a work-readiness or career education program for the non–college bound. In other instances, state mandates and academic assessments associated with education reform are driving teachers and schools back to a narrow view of what constitutes academic rigor, thus lessening the potential impact of school-to-career principles.

Other states, however, are taking the approach that school-to-career initiatives should be integrated as part of a broad education reform agenda. (Oregon, Maryland, Kentucky, and New Hampshire are examples.) In some states legislation governing education incorporates key school-to-work principles. Beyond the level of rhetoric, such integration becomes real when states put a priority on contextual and applied learning in allocating resources, setting standards, and helping teachers grow professionally.

Concretely, this means—as in Kentucky—state assessments that emphasize applied as well as academic learning and—as in New Hampshire—flexibility in using vocational and school-to-career monies to support pedagogical and school organizational strategies like the ones we discuss here. The guidelines for professional development, the graduation requirements, and the range and types of assessments are important signals as to whether both hands are clapping.

Even where there is poor alignment at the state level, local partnerships usually have leeway in how they spend school-to-work dollars, 90 percent of which pass through the state to local or regional entities. Such partnerships can decide to emphasize school-to-career as a vehicle for engaging a broader range of students in learning the core academic content.

For example, the Cranberry School-to-Career Partnership, Inc., in southeastern Massachusetts, which encompasses twenty school districts, solicits competitive proposals from the schools in the partnership directed at "capturing the concepts of school-to-career within the context of educational reform." Curriculum cluster teams from the districts have been awarded grants to do such integrative projects as linking electronics to the study of oceanography or connecting the study of world languages to a health careers pathway.

In large urban districts, community leadership councils such as those described earlier become a key to mobilizing business and school support for this kind of innovative use of school-to-career funds.

With so much variation among states, the survival of Essential school principles and school-to-career approaches depends more than ever on clarity of purpose and strong support at the local level. In addressing both the carrots and the sticks coming from the state, districts and communities must make the strong case that the very opportunity to learn for many students depends on structured access to community or workplace settings where they can see the connection between academic concepts and real-world applications.

Continuing the Conversation

The current moment in education is increasingly dominated by notions of standards-based reform. Almost every state has crafted new and higher standards that its students must meet. Most states have introduced new assessment mechanisms by instituting statewide tests that measure progress of students, schools, and districts toward meeting the standards. The fate of both Essential school and school-to-career ideas will rest on whether the definition of standards that prevail focuses on traditional academic content, as measured by multiple choice and short-answer tests, or on new combinations of academic and applied learning, demonstrated through projects and performances that reveal habits of mind and work.

Two aspects of the standards movement—the nature of state assessments and the pressure to teach to the test—challenge at least the short-term diffusion of the kinds of pedagogy and school organization championed by Essential school and school-to-career educators. For reasons of simplicity, cost, and validity, most states have introduced standardized tests that reward the coverage of traditional subject matter content. These instruments rarely move beyond testing students' knowledge and toward assessing their ability to retain and use information in different settings and to demonstrate the skills and habits of mind and work needed in the adult world. The tests do not incorporate such cross-cutting skills as communication, teamwork, and other skills people need to succeed; performance-based assessments are the exception rather than the rule. State assessments focus on what students should know, not what they can do—or, more important, *will* do when faced with a new situation or real problem.

Kentucky, a leader in raising standards and introducing a statewide assessment system around those standards, provides an illustration of this problem. The state initially designed an assessment system that incorporated performances, portfolios, and other less-standardized indicators. After a few years, faced with high costs and legal challenges, the state retreated toward simpler, more standardized paper-and-pencil tests, with an increasing number of multiple-choice items. And few states have even tried to be as flexible and creative as Kentucky.

Teachers feel pressured to teach to such standardized tests, which leads them away from taking risks and from trying non-traditional approaches to curriculum and classroom activities. It takes considerable courage for educators to proceed with project-based or work-based learning programs before enough research exists to bear out their conviction that test scores will not suffer from these approaches.

At the same time, the initial rush by states to introduce new standards and assessments is largely over. Now states will have to assess the results of their work, fine-tune or revamp their tools and systems, and address the inevitable problems—not the least of which is the unacceptably high failure rates on the new tests. This reassessment leaves an increased opportunity to reopen the dialogue about the shape and purpose of the American high school and about the effectiveness of strategies that combine rigor and relevance.

Essential schools and school-to-career initiatives are creating new and important conversations about school reform. As teachers from Essential schools and school-to-career programs join forces to provide both rigor and relevance in secondary education, student learning will increase and deepen at every point on the spectrum of academic achievement. And as that work continues, it will acquire an even more important potential—to transform beleaguered schools and communities, creating new contexts in which young people work with and learn from adults both in and out of school. It is time for these two movements to declare themselves forcefully and publicly as an essential school-to-career coalition.

Resources for Practitioners

Organizations

ACADEMY FOR EDUCATION DEVELOPMENT AND DEFENSE TECHNOLO-
GIES, INC., coordinates technical assistance to states receiving federal
school-to-work funds: www.stw.ed.gov

AMERICAN YOUTH POLICY FORUM has publications on youth development and school-to-work issues: 1001 Connecticut Ave. NW, Ste. 719,
Washington, D.C. 20036; (202) 775-9731.

CHANGING THE SUBJECT: THE NEW URBAN HIGH SCHOOL is a demonstration project of the Big Picture Company and the U.S. Department
of Education: 118 Magazine St., Cambridge, Mass. 02139;
(617) 492-5335; www.bpic.org

THE COALITION OF ESSENTIAL SCHOOLS is a national network of schools
and centers engaged in restructuring and redesigning schools to promote better student learning and achievement. National Office: 1814
Franklin St., Ste. 700, Oakland, Calif. 94612; (510) 433-1451,
FAX: (510) 433-1455.

FOOTHILL ASSOCIATES provides technical assistance and research on
partnership academies: 230 Main St., Nevada City, Calif. 95959;
(916) 265-8116.

JOBS FOR THE FUTURE works nationally with schools, districts, and communities to design, create, and assess school-to-career learning:
88 Broad St., 8th Floor, Boston, Mass. 02110; (617) 728-4446;
e-mail: info@jff.org

MANPOWER DEMONSTRATION RESEARCH CORPORATION designs and tests education- and employment-related programs for disadvantaged populations: 16 East 34th St., New York, N.Y. 10016; (212) 532-3200.

NATIONAL ACADEMY FOUNDATION in New York networks more than 170 career academy programs nationwide: 235 Park Ave. South, 7th Floor, New York, N.Y. 10003; (212) 420-8400.

NATIONAL CENTER FOR RESEARCH IN VOCATIONAL EDUCATION is a federally funded research center that generates publications on issues of learning, work experience, and professional development in career and vocational education: 2030 Addison St., Ste. 500, Berkeley, Calif. 94720; (800) 762-4093.

NEW WAYS WORKERS acts as a national broker for school districts, community organizations, businesses, and other groups to provide work-based educational experiences for students: 785 Market St., Ste. 950, San Francisco, Calif. 94103; (415) 995-9860.

NORTHWEST REGIONAL EDUCATIONAL LABORATORY has fine materials from its Education and Work program, Integrated Workplace Learning Project, and more: 101 S.W. Main, Ste. 500, Portland, Oreg. 97204; (503) 275-9500 or (800) 547-6339; e-mail: info@nwrel.org; www.nwrel.org

PROJECT-BASED LEARNING NETWORK connects educators interested in project-based learning, school-to-career initiatives, and education reform: Autodesk Foundation, 111 McInnis Pkwy., San Rafael, Calif. 94903; (415) 507-5664.

WISE INDIVIDUALIZED SENIOR EXPERIENCE (WISE) SERVICES help schools organize project-based learning as transition to life beyond high school: Vic Leviatin, 29 Old Tarrytown Rd., White Plains, N.Y. 10603; (914) 428-1968.

WORKING TO LEARN, a project of TERC Communications, develops curriculum materials and runs workshops to strengthen the quality of work-based learning: 2067 Massachusetts Ave., Cambridge, Mass. 02140; (617) 547-0430.

Readings

Allen, L., Hogan, C., and Steinberg, A. *Knowing and Doing: Connecting Learning and Work.* Providence, R.I.: Regional Educational Laboratory at Brown University, forthcoming.

Alongi, A., Arora, S., Hogan, C., Steinberg, A., with Margaret Vickers. *Creating Quality Student Projects for Studies in Health Care Careers: A Portable Action Lab.* Boston: Jobs for the Future, 1997.

American Federation of Teachers. *Reaching the Next Step: How School-to-Career Can Help Students Reach High Academic Standards and Prepare for Good Jobs.* Washington, D.C.: American Federation of Teachers, 1997.

Bailey, T., and Merritt, D. *School-to-Work for the College Bound.* New York: Institute on Education and the Economy, Teachers College, Columbia University, 1997.

Bailey, T. (ed.). *Learning to Work: Employer Involvement in School-to-Work Transition Programs.* Washington, D.C.: The Brookings Institution, 1995.

Berger, R. "A Culture of Quality: A Reflection on Practice." Occasional Paper Series, no. 1. Providence, R.I.: Annenberg Institute for School Reform, 1996.

The Big Picture Company. *The New Urban High School: A Practitioner's Guide,* 1998. Available from Standard Modern Fulfillment Center, P.O. Box 4971, Brockton, Mass. 02303; (800) 742-4123.

Bottoms, G., and Sharpe, D. *Teaching for Understanding Through Integration of Academic and Technical Education.* Atlanta, Ga.: Southern Regional Education Board.

Business Roundtable. *A Business Leader's Guide to Setting Academic Standards.* Washington, D.C.: Business Roundtable, 1996.

Center for Learning, Technology, and Work. *Integrating Science and the Workplace: A Curriculum User's Guide.* Andover, Mass.: Center for Learning, Technology, and Work, 1995.

Committee for Economic Development. *American Workers and Economic Change.* Washington, D.C.: Committee for Economic Development, 1996.

Committee for Economic Development. *Connecting Inner-City Youth to the World of Work.* Washington, D.C.: Committee for Economic Development, 1996.

Cushman, K. "What's 'Essential' about Learning in the World of Work?" *Horace,* 1997, 14(1).

Cushman, K. *The Collected Horace: Theory and Practice in Essential Schools.* 5 vols. Oakland, Calif.: Coalition of Essential Schools, 1998.

de Leeuw, D., and others. *Examples of Integrated Academic and Vocational Curriculum From High School Academies in the Oakland Unified School District.* Berkeley, Calif.: National Center for Research in Vocational Education, 1992.

Dewey, J. "Democracy and Education." In J. A. Boydston (ed.), *John Dewey: The Middle Works, 1899–1924.* Carbondale, Ill.: Southern Illinois University Press, 1980.

Freire, P. "Cultural Action for Freedom." Reprinted in *Harvard Educational Review, 68*(4).

Gardner, H. *Frames of Mind.* New York: Basic Books, 1983.

Gardner, H. *The Unschooled Mind: How Children Think and How Schools Should Teach.* New York: Basic Books, 1991.

Goldberger, S., and Kazis, R. *Revitalizing High Schools: What the School-to-Career Movement Can Contribute.* Boston: Jobs for the Future, 1995.

Goldberger, S., Kazis, R., and O'Flanagan, M. K. *Learning Through Work: Designing and Implementing Quality Workaday Learning for High School Students.* New York: Manpower Demonstration Research Corporation, 1994.

Grobe, T., Nahas, J., and Steinbrueck, K. *Work-Based Learning: A Best Practices Guide.* Waltham, Mass.: Center for Human Resources, Brandeis University, 1996.

Grubb, W. N. "Reconstructing Urban Schools with Work-Centered Education." *Education and Urban Society,* May 1995.

Grubb, W. N. (ed.). *Education Through Occupations in American High Schools, Volumes I and II.* New York: Teachers College Press, 1995.

Hamilton, M. A., and Hamilton, S. F. *Learning Well at Work: Choices for Quality.* Washington, D.C.: National School-to-Work Office, 1997.

Hamilton, S. *Apprenticeship for Adulthood.* New York: Free Press, 1990.

Holzer, H. *What Employers Want: Job Prospects for Less-Educated Workers.* New York: Russell Sage Foundation, 1996.

Jobs for the Future. *School-to-Work Toolkits: Building a Local Program and Building a Statewide System.* Boston: Jobs for the Future, 1994.

Kazis, R., and Kopp, H. *Both Sides Now: New Directions in Promoting Work and Learning for Disadvantaged Youth.* Baltimore, Md.: Annie E. Casey Foundation, 1997.

Kopp, H., and Kazis, R. *Promising Practices: A Study of Ten School-to-Career Programs.* Boston: Jobs for the Future, 1995.

Krechevsky, M., and Seidel, S. "Minds at Work: Applying Multiple Intelligences in the Classroom." In R. J. Sternberg and W. Williams (eds.), *Intelligence, Instruction, and Assessment.* Hillsdale, N.J.: Erlbaum, 1998.

Mednick, A., and Cousins, E. (eds.). *Fieldwork: An Expeditionary Learning Outward Bound Reader, Volumes I and II.* Dubuque, Iowa: Kendall/Hunt, 1996.

Meier, D. *The Power of Their Ideas: Lessons for America from a Small School in Harlem.* Boston: Beacon Press, 1995.

Murnane, R. J., and Levy, F. *Teaching the New Basic Skills: Principles for Edu-*

cating Children to Thrive in a Changing Economy. New York: Free Press, 1996.

National Center for Research in Vocational Education. *Legislative Principles for Career-Related Education and Training: What Research Supports.* Berkeley, Calif.: National Center for Research in Vocational Education, 1995.

Newmann, F., Secada, W. G., and Wehlage, G. *A Guide to Authentic Instruction and Assessment: Vision, Standards, and Scoring.* Madison, Wis.: Center on Organization and Restructuring of Schools, 1995.

Newmann, F., and Wehlage, G. *Successful School Restructuring: A Report to the Public and Educators.* Madison, Wis.: Center on Organization and Restructuring of Schools, 1995.

Northwest Regional Educational Laboratory. *Connections: Products and Services for Linking Work and Learning.* Portland, Oreg.: Northwest Regional Educational Lab, 1996.

Olson, L. *The School-to-Work Revolution: How Employers and Educators Are Joining Forces to Prepare Tomorrow's Skilled Workforce.* Reading, Mass.: Addison-Wesley, 1997.

Pauly, E., Kopp, H., and Haimson, J. *Home-Grown Lessons: Innovative Programs Linking Work and School.* San Francisco: Jossey-Bass, 1995.

Pedraza, R., Pauly, E., and Kopp, H. *Home-Grown Progress: The Evolution of Innovative School-to-Work Programs.* New York: Manpower Demonstration Research Corporation, 1997.

Resnick, L. "Presidential Address: Learning In School and Out." *Educational Researcher,* 1987, 16.

Riordan, R., and others. *Seeing the Future: A Planning Guide for High Schools.* Providence, R.I.: The Big Picture Company, 1999.

Rogers, S., and Graham, S. *The High Performance Tool Box.* Evergreen, Colo.: Peak Learning Systems, 1997.

Secretary's Commission on Achieving Necessary Skills, U.S. Department of Labor. *What Work Requires of Schools: A SCANS Report for America 2000.* Washington, D.C.: U.S. Department of Labor, 1991.

Sizer, T. *Horace's Compromise: The Dilemma of the American High School.* Boston: Houghton Mifflin, 1984.

Sizer, T. *Horace's School: Redesigning the American High School.* Boston: Houghton Mifflin, 1992.

Sizer, T. *Horace's Hope: What Works for the American High School.* Boston: Houghton Mifflin, 1996.

Stasz, C. *The Economic Imperative Behind School Reform: A Review of the Literature.* Berkeley, Calif.: National Center for Research in Vocational Education, 1996.

Steinberg, A. *Real Learning, Real Work: School-to-Work as High School Reform.* New York: Routledge, 1997.

Steinberg, A. "Making Schoolwork More Like Real Work." *Harvard Education Letter,* 1997, *13*(2), 1–6.

Stern, D., Raby, M., and Dayton, C. *Career Academics: Partnerships for Reconstructing American High Schools.* San Francisco: Jossey-Bass, 1992.

Udall, D., and Mednick, A. (eds.). *Journeys Through Our Classrooms.* Dubuque, Iowa: Kendall/Hunt, 1996.

Vickers, M. "Clapping With One Hand: Why the School-to-Work and Standards Movements Should Be Linked." *Harvard Education Letter, 12*(2).

Video Productions

Central Park East Secondary School. *Graduation by Portfolio: Performance-Based Assessment at Central Park East Secondary* School. New York: Center for Collaborative Education. Videotape.

Jobs for the Future and the American Youth Policy Forum. *School-to-Careers: Connecting Youth to the Future.* Boston: Jobs for the Future, 1995. Videotape.

Hamilton, S. F., and Hamilton, M. A. *Projects for School and Work: Meeting the Standards: Cornell Youth and Work Program.* Ithaca, N.Y.: Cornell University Media Services Resource Center. Videotape.

Index

C